Charles M. Olsen is director of Project Base Church, a part of the ministry of The Institute of Church Renewal in Atlanta.

Prior to joining ICR, he was with the Board of National Ministries of the Presbyterian Church, U.S., as director of Congregational Evangelism/Mission Development with particular responsibility for lay renewal, evangelism strategy, witness training, and small group development.

In preparation for writing The Base Church, he spent the summer of 1972 in Europe researching the various forms of Christian community in England, Scotland, France, Belgium, Germany, and Switzerland.

Olsen has also developed two cassette resources for Forum House, "Skills in Communicating Good News" and "The Church in Small Groups." He was a contributing author to Rebels in the Church, published by Word, Inc., in 1970, and has written articles for denominational publications.

He received his M.Div. from Pittsburgh Seminary. During his years in the pastorate in Pennsylvania, he directed a one-year renewal project for the Beaver-Butler Presbytery.

THE BASE CHURCH

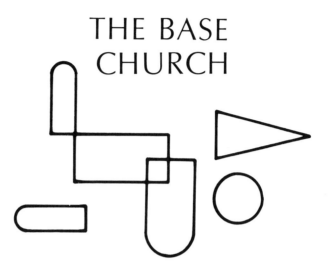

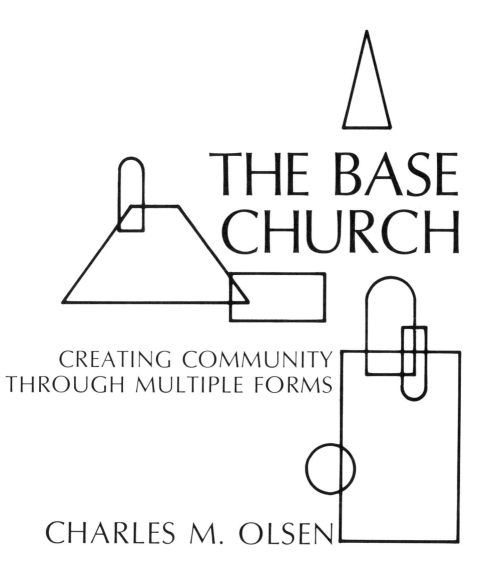

THE BASE CHURCH

CREATING COMMUNITY THROUGH MULTIPLE FORMS

CHARLES M. OLSEN

FORUM HOUSE/Publishers

Atlanta

Printed in the United States of America

First printing June 1973
Second printing January 1974

Library of Congress catalog card number: 73-81260
ISBN: 0-913618-13-6

A list of reference sources for which the publishers give grateful ac-
knowledgment can be found at the end of the book.

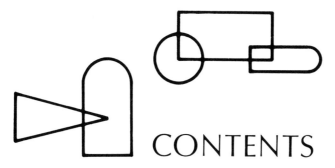

CONTENTS

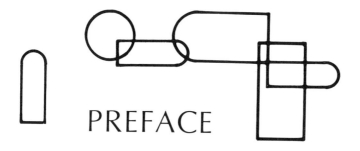

PREFACE

PILGRIMAGE TO BASE COMMUNITY

When I was a child . . .
  I knew, felt, breathed *community*
    on a family farm
      close to the animals
      close to the soil
    in an extended family
      with two dozen aunts and uncles
      and scores of cousins
    all within a 20-mile radius
      of a small farming community.

Today my children . . .
  go to school with hundreds
  play mostly organized sports
  have no relatives within a thousand miles
  see their friends move in and out
    every three or so years.

Since leaving home to go to college
  I have known *community* . . .
    four different times!
  In 20 years I have accumulated
    four different sets of friends.

Community was ready-made
    in a small college
    and in seminary.

In the pastorate, *community*
  did not come easily —
    too many roles to play:
      Be strong!
      Be good!
      Be pure!
      Be smart!
      Be kind!
      Be loving!
      Be humorous!
        Even when I didn't feel like it.

But then I discovered a very human *community*
  of pastors.
    There we shared our struggles
      our weakness
      our humanity
      our vulnerability.
    There we were alive
      with feeling
      with love
      with joy.

I discovered I could be weak,
  and human.
People could then love
  and reach out to me.
I tasted *community*
  with people who prayed,
    cared,
  and loved 'til it hurt.
It was a new day
  something like a fresh breeze.
  A taste of heaven?
  A taste of what "church" is?

Transition to a new job
   in a denominational office brought
      new possibilities
         for team/staff relations
      new insights to the church as "system."
Transition to the role of parishioner in the local congregation
   produced frustration.
      Instead of being an active participant in worship
         I was a passive listener.
      Instead of creatively thinking
         I mulled over secondhand thoughts.
      Instead of being caught up in the community
         my children were separated four ways in church school
         my wife was pulled into
            activities for women.
      I worshiped in a sea of strangers

The church tries with
   name tags!
   coffee!
   fellowship time!
   recreation!
   visitation!
But community calls for . . .
   Weeping with those who weep
   Rejoicing with those who are happy
   Bearing heavy burdens
   Praying for a brother
   Praising God together.

Then God's gifts came to me through a small house church
   in people hungry for bread
      broken bread
      shared bread.

We shared weekly
  around new bread
  on the floor
  with our children.

We sang
  and danced
    and prayed
      and laughed
        and wept
          and played
            and studied
  and praised God!

Our life
  bloomed in resurrection faith
      dying in risk and pain
      waiting for Easter light
      rejoicing in the Holy Spirit
        whose gift was
              Community!

The Spirit blew a dream.
  A vision was born.

I saw seeds of a new church
    growing in Europe
        in India
        in America.

Small house groups of Christians
    gathered
        to learn, love, and worship
    scattered to work, witness, and serve.

Being the church
    with full marks
        yet not alone or underground.

But clustered together
       affirming their unity
       celebrating their diversity
       living accountable
              to "the brothers."

Jesus is Lord
       of the church
              no matter what the varying
                     forms may be!
       That is given.

The Holy Spirit
       calls the church
              to be and do.
       That is promised.

In the small group
       one can experience the gospel
              grace
              affirmation
              pardon
              freedom
              support
              power
              service.
       That has been proven.

Words say so much,
   yet so little.
Meanings have shades of difference
   conditioned by our experience.

So we go on a search
   for words
       which communicate
              and capture meaning.

This book is about a new style of church
    which is built
        on the life of authentic
            Christian communities.
            (house churches
                task groups
                cell groups . . .)

Our search takes us to the dictionary
    and there focuses
        on the words
            base and *basis*.

There we see *base* as:

(1)   The bottom on which
            anything stands.

        We stand on Christ
            who lives in his people
                two or three gathered.

        He is the foundation upon which
            the building is erected.
            We are the present-day
            living stones
            arranged *together*!

(2)   The fundamental principle.

        We are the body
            of Christ
        Living as the extension
            of his body in the world.
        We are unique and different
            hands
            eyes
            feet
            ears
        Yet functioning in love
            together!

(3)   The principal ingredient.

The Spirit calls us
                gathers us
                empowers us
                guides us
                comforts us
                teaches us
and brings us into unity
                together!

(4)   A starting place.

Jesus gathered a small group.
A small group
    prayed and waited
        for Pentecost.

House churches launched
    a world-wide
        missionary effort.

"Get *together*,
get changed,
and get going!"

(5)   A secure place.

An equipping station
    which heals
                supports
                trains
                strategizes,
Does not do so for its own sake
But for a mission to be engaged in
                together!

(6)   Inferior, low, despised, humble.

Yes, this also describes us.
    Not much power
    not much wealth
    not much wisdom.

But God
          confounds the wise
          and uses the base and low
          (even the foolish)
                    to reconcile the world
                    to bring us
                              together!

We will then talk about:

    Base groups
          the building blocks of the church
    Base community
          the style of life together
    Base church
          the total system
          which incorporates
                    wide options of community
                    bearing unity
                              accountability
                              authority
                    with the brothers
                              together!

So what is needful today?
          A forthright strategy
          of church renewal
          which will point the way
          which will lay a solid base for the church
                    where we can experience *base community*!

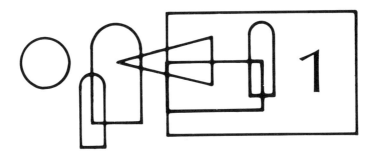

TOWARD A NEW BASE
FOR THE CHURCH

The whole congregation gathers at once (at least the "faith-ful" do), lines up in rows facing the front, listens to a leader, departs the sanctuary complimenting the leader and engaging in polite chit-chat with one another, then returns home. Is this the conventional picture of the church today? I believe it is. The "standard" congregation exists as the dominant form of Christian community.

The Time Is Now

The church has changed little since the Reformation, but the need for reformation did not end in the sixteenth century. Reformation must remain alive, for the church claims to be an ever-reforming body. Now is the time for us to take a fresh look at our church structures — a time to ask ourselves, "What forms of the church are best suited for the latter part of the twentieth century? On what forms will the church of the twenty-first century be constructed?"

John Gardner, in *Self-Renewal*, defines the self-renewing organization as one that constantly changes its structure in response to changing needs. The world changes. Politics, educa-tion, and industry change with rapid acceleration. But can or should the church adjust to the world's change?

Some aspects of the church are constants; they do not change. The church is rooted in the tradition of Jesus, the apostles, and the prophets. It finds its life in Jesus Christ and gathers itself under the Word and the sacraments. Its mission is always directed outward to the world for ministry, service, and the pursuit of justice. Yet, the forms in which gathering, nurturing, and ministry take place must necessarily change and vary. We cannot borrow a sixteenth-century form and merely spruce it up for our day!

A group of Methodists in Atlanta struggled with the question of form and decided they would like to experiment with a test congregation. In their letter of request to their bishop, they stated:

> Whereas the functions which grow out of the essence of the church do not change, the form, or structure, in which these functions express themselves must change. Form, or structures, of the congregation must be appropriate for the culture and the situation in which the church exists. The question, therefore, becomes: What shape shall the church take? What is the most appropriate structure for any given period in history?

After much study and discussion, the group concluded that a house church which would meet on Sunday evenings with shared leadership was the form to pursue.

Countless other groups of Christians struggle with the same questions. Forces at work in the world and in the church prick and prod us into a restlessness over our present structures. Things as they are in the typical residentially based congregation are being called into question.

Forces in the world push the church to review and reevaluate its structures.

The most striking characteristic of our age is mobility. One family in four moves every year. People migrate from rural areas to urban areas, which themselves burgeon into megalopolises. One can whisk across town to a department store, sporting event, or favorite restaurant in a rapid transit car or personal automobile, or jet to a holiday weekend on a southern beach.

Change becomes the basic building block of life. A man may change his occupation three to four times.

Extended weekends, elongated vacations, and early retirement make mobile-home living a live option for the modern nomad. Increasing numbers of persons, especially retirees, have no permanent address. Housing patterns are geared for people on the move. Of all living units built in 1971, 56 percent were apartments and mobile homes, contrasted with less than 10 percent in 1950. Of housing being started in metropolitan Atlanta, more than 65 percent is in the form of multi-family units (within the city limits, 85 percent). People on the move don't have time to bother with a lawn or plumbing — sometimes not even with neighbors.

Where does this mobility leave the parish congregation? It leaves them chasing the welcome wagon as a way to scout out prospects. The church enrolls new members, but says good-bye before the newcomers are settled. Recruitment becomes a bother — correcting address plates, figuring out how to gain access to people in new apartments, and puzzling over ways to keep attendance up during vacation months and beautiful weekends.

And where does this mobility leave the *person*? His roots in community do not run deep. He is hungry for "family" and intimacy, yet finds that his relationships are temporary. He is driven to shallow impersonalism and deep loneliness. Vance Packard describes it well in *A Nation of Strangers*. The title says it all.

Communication bombards us from every side. Television brings news of violent change into our living rooms. Computers put new information at our fingertips. No one place (library, church building) or person (teacher, clergyman) has a corner on the information market. The media get to our senses. Sight and sound, as captured on film, are far more expressive than the printed word or prepared speech. People no longer have to go to church to get the latest views, even about religion.

The existence of pollution, racism, and war call into question the value system with which the church in America has been comfortable. Countercultural voices question church structures which are impotent on crucial issues and often do not foster a climate in which people can appropriate deeper human values.

Growing dissatisfaction with decisions made by a distant leadership stirs people either to drop out or to gain the right to participate in the governing structure. New styles of community life and organizational development push participation in the decision-making process to a lower level and broader base. Experience-oriented small groups proliferate outside the church — in industry, education, and countless personal growth centers. The *world* has discovered a secret of the first-century church which most *congregations* have lost. Bernard Gunther titles his book on personal and interpersonal growth *What To Do 'Til The Messiah Comes*. Many of the exercises which he describes are closely related to the church's sacraments and rituals. I suppose anyone can read out of the title what he wants, so I interpret it as "what to do until the church gets with it and really becomes the church; in the meantime, the world will point the way." Participation, humanness, feelings, intimacy, and shared decisions characterize a new discipline which is rising outside the church. And just think — the church has for centuries been sitting on the blueprint for human community!

Forces within the church, too, push for a fresh look at church structures.

Always, the first ingredient for change is dissatisfaction with the present state of affairs. I hesitate to get caught playing the "What's Wrong with the Church" game, because the purpose of this book is one of construction — namely, to advocate some positive directions and transitional steps for structuring a more nearly authentic church base. However, since dissatisfaction breeds change, let's take a quick look at some symptoms of unrest before we move on.

Attendance continues to decline and memberships grow older. The average American is twenty-seven years old and the average is dropping. In contrast, the average church member is forty years old and the average is rising. Large churches, particularly, find it difficult to maintain attendance. The inactive member and the dropout draw attention and concern. Most observers conjecture that those dropping out are in the eighteen to twenty-four age range. A closer look, however, reveals an alarming number in the thirty-five to fifty bracket. These do not leave because the church has offended them or asked too much of them; rather, they depart because the church has failed to engage them. People get bored by passive membership and insignificant participation.

The grip which professionals hold on the church alienates the rank and file, who feel left out and powerless. Jeffrey Hadden documents this well in *The Gathering Storm in the Churches*. The gap between lay and clergy viewpoints produces an atmosphere in which the only way the layman can be heard is to reduce his giving, and that he does! Every major denominational agency feels the pinch. Thus, the mandate is to find a church base in which the laity can exercise power and participate.

The laity doesn't have a corner on discontent. National publications continue to print stories of clergymen dropping out. A church system which demands too much of a pastor forces him into a role and squeezes out his creative energy. As a Presbyterian clergyman attending Presbytery meetings, I hear names of pastors read out who have "demitted the ministry." Does their decision suggest a loss of faith or a loss of love for God and the church? No. I know many of these men. They are not heretics. They are not incompetent. Among them are the most able servants of the church. They love God, their fellow men, and even the church. But they feel that the present church system is eating them alive!

Another force for reevaluation is the religious revival outside the church. A few years ago, a student attending a Billy Graham revival carried a sign reading, "Jesus, YES; Christianity, NO!" He was attracted to Jesus but repulsed by the church. The "Jesus Revolution" grew up alien to institutional structures, and its ecumenical character leaves sectarian denominations on the outside, looking in. Many corporate expressions of the Jesus People (baptismal celebrations, prayer groups, communes) stretch and thus challenge those of the church, but rarely have the two systems interlocked.

Look at the polarization within the church. The Roman Catholic Church has learned better how to tolerate and incorporate diversity than have Protestant denominations. Protestants tend to get locked into a posture of maximum uniformity. Now

6

the polarization which has long been felt at the denominational level is being felt in the local congregation. Traditionally, the pattern has been "everyone in step behind the leader." The result is, we do not know how to handle diversity. Our structures have not been constructed to embrace pluralism, and now we are paying the consequences. Consider, for example, a certain 4,000-member church which failed to raise its budget. The conservatives withheld money because of what the liberals were doing, and the liberals withheld money because of what the conservatives *weren't* doing! To be meaningful, emerging church forms will have to incorporate, bless, and build upon diversity of life, belief, and ministry.

Over the past two decades, countless revival schemes have been constructed to pump new life into the existing system, but the central problem — the monolithic structure — prevails. The renewal parade has included new church-school curricula, visitation evangelism, relevant preaching, social action, organizational development, clustering, liturgical renewal, lay renewal, small groups — and *construction*! One "successful" pastor told me: "To grow, a church has to have clear goals. Not being able to find any, we build buildings! A poor goal is always better than no goal. Just keep them a little in debt and continue to build. You can't miss!"

Although most of the renewal attempts have been appropriate for their time and have served a need, they are limited in what they can do. The Reformation model of congregation, with its authority/dependency style of functioning and family-oriented approach to enrollment, imposes formidable limits. The *base* of the congregation is simply a collection of individuals or families.

The How Is Now

I advocate a church "base" which consists of dynamic, cellular groups of people who gather out of their common experience of Christ to learn and live out his love together. I advocate a church "base" which is a connectional organism of living cells of Christians. I choose to call these small groups "base" groups. Base groups provide the foundation for any church superstructure. Base groups reveal an essence of the church's life, where people experience and share unearned love. Base groups function together in a unified, interlocking manner.

Jesus gathered around him a small group of twelve men into whom he could pour his life, thoughts, and emotions. The New Testament church gathered people who had a common experience. Love flowed into their lives; fear, guilt, and isolation flowed out. A new freedom and boldness possessed them. They discovered God in transformation through Jesus Christ. Their experience shouts from the pages of the New Testament, and it became the foundation of a church which was "born," not blueprinted.

The house church became the basic unit of Christian fellowship. ("House" — an open, informal, face-to-face context for at-homeness, intimacy, and warmth. Plus "church" — a community of God's called-out people who are connected to his activity in history.)

Today, for some persons, the term "house church" conjures up anticongregational, anticlerical, anti-institutional images. More popularly, it is viewed as a uniform style of small church groups which lack an edifice orientation.

When I use the term "house church" in this book, I mean a small, intimate grouping of Christians who meet for worship and ministry. The *forms* may vary (the group may not even meet in a house, but rather in a borrowed or rented meeting room); the *style*, however, is constant. The house church which functions within multiple forms comes close to my understanding of "base-church" community. In fact, I may occasionally use the terms "house church" and "base church" interchangeably, even though in meaning "base" is more inclusive than "house."

What do people see when they encounter the word "church"? I'm sure that some visualize buildings with stained-glass windows, institutions that are oiled to run smoothly, and leaders who are schooled in the latest communication and management skills. But I insist that church must be more than this: It must be a dynamic base consisting of a network of gatherings of two or three together.

Emil Brunner wrote *The Misunderstanding of the Church* out

of the European scene of 1952. The adage "European trends hit America twenty years later" propels his thesis into the American scene today. Brunner describes the spontaneous, organic life of the house church unit as the *ecclesia* of the New Testament. *Ecclesia* is the fellowship of Christian believers who participate together in a community life. It is not to be equated with the institution which we call "church" today.

> The meaning of the Ecclesia is what we recognized from the New Testament as its characteristic essence: communion with God through Jesus Christ, and rooted in this and springing from it, communion or brotherhood with man. The oneness of communion with Christ and communion with man is the characteristic mark of the Ecclesia . . . . No true *Ecclesia* can be made out of twenty ecclesiastical institutions; Christian fellowship can spring only from spiritual knowledge of Christ, which implies the will to brotherhood in Christ. For in Christ recognition of the truth and the will to fellowship with man are one. Only faith which proves its reality by love is true faith.[1]

The Apostle Paul describes the church as a "body" with living cells, differing in functional parts, coordinated by love, and all under the control of Christ, who is the head. I affirm base groups as living and dynamic cells *not separated from a head*! There is a trend to label as a "Christian fellowship" any group which assembles for the purpose of encounter, personal growth, or personal support. Yet, a line must be drawn. It is true that understanding, acceptance, belonging, and security are real life-nurturing qualities and they are experienced in the small group, whether it is a temporary or long-term group. Further, it must be acknowledged that the church needs to listen and learn from the small-group movement. I would, however, insist that the church — whether represented by a small group or a huge congregation — must give proper attention to theology. Not *all* small groups do this.

My own experience in well-conducted encounter groups has been most positive; however, I have usually gone away feeling that something was missing. The missing element is an affirma-

---

[1]Emil Brunner, *The Misunderstanding of the Church* (London: Lutterworth Press, 1952), pp. 107, 111.

tion of Christ and a celebration of his presence. I confess that his presence is a mystery and is, as Brunner says, all wrapped up in relationships with the brothers. Yet, the intentional commitment of one's will to Jesus Christ and his way provides a theological dimension which the so-called "encounter" groups frequently lack. The base group covenant combines the best of the two worlds. Members of the base group stick together as humans, yet they are joined to one another through Christ.

> Instead, by speaking the truth in a spirit of love, we must grow up in every way to Christ, who is the head. Under his control all the different parts of the body fit together, and the whole body is held together by every joint with which it is provided. So when each separate part works as it should, the whole body grows and builds itself up through love.
>
> Ephesians 4:15, 16 (TEV)

The base group functions as a living organism with Christ at the center. But if the base group is to be an authentic unit upon which the church builds, it must deal openly with the human dilemma. I hear many exponents prescribe small groups as a panacea for the renewal of the church. But be prepared! People will bring to the base group the same hang-ups, insecurity, frustrations, guilt, and idiosyncrasies which they bring to the traditional church. In fact, in the base group these problems surface faster and with more impact because few hiding places exist. The difference (and hope) of the base group lies in its capacity for dealing with the human dilemma on a relational, as well as intellectual, level. People's real, feeling-level agenda becomes the group's agenda. Theology can be experienced as well as talked about.

Doctrinally, the church views man as being a strange mixture, both creative and destructive, both saint and sinner. We know our weakness, selfishness, and will to power, but we don't know quite what to do about them. So we carry in our gut all our negative feelings, convinced that we are not quite acceptable to ourselves, to others, or to God. In our efforts to establish identity and gain power, we pull all kinds of tricks. We perform for others to earn their acceptance. We remain unable to accept ourselves, whereupon we "try harder."

The church's business is to *proclaim* the good news and *be* the good news to man at the point of his deepest need. Words like "deliverance," "freedom," "pardon," "grace," and "salvation" must become operative within the cellular base church, for man's central need does not change. Our common unacceptableness is accepted by God's amazing love. That is the tradition upon which we stand.

I have been puzzled by the seeming paradox of people desperately crying to belong to an intimate community while, at the same time, they are possessed by a haunting fear. How can a person desire something, yet be afraid of the thing desired? My new perspective sees people who want to be accepted but are afraid that their reaching out will ultimately result in rejection — they fear that the group will find them unacceptable once it gets to know them.

But the good news of God's love, as it is declared and shared in community, opens the door so that I can risk sharing who I am — both the good and bad of my humanness. I can begin to share my history and claim my uniqueness, and feel good about it. The base community says, "You're okay. You matter to God and to us. You don't have to wear a mask here. We love and accept you. We will carry your burdens." When the base community says these things, liberation floods my life. I move from fear to trust, from role to personhood, from bondage to salvation. Miracles of change come into my life. Feelings of self-worth are activated, and this sense of self-worth produces a new style of openness and loving.

Fear blocks community, but "perfect love casts our fear" and community becomes a reality. My human dilemma has been touched by God's grace. The group has not protected me from guilt or from death, but has made it possible for me to acknowledge my inadequacy and guilt and to permit Christ to help me bear my burden.

The Holy Spirit lives in and brings life to the church. He gives gifts for a total "body" ministry. Authentic evangelism happens. Brunner observes,

> Where the Holy Spirit is, there is the Christian communion.
> And the Holy Spirit is not otherwise there than as the Spirit

given to the community. Therefore the community as bearer of the Word and Spirit of Christ precedes the individual believer. One does not first believe and then join the fellowship: but one becomes a believer just because one shares in a gift vouchsafed to the fellowship.[2]

Pastors tell me that more conversions of an authentic and lasting nature take place in small groups than in any other facet of church programming. And some uninitiated persons would be surprised to learn that the group exerts little overt pressure to "convert." Telling one's own story of doubt and fear may launch an adventure into commitment.

Robert Raines, in *New Life in the Church*, records the experience of small group life in the Aldersgate Methodist Church of Cleveland. He affirms that koinonia (fellowship) provides the context for conversion.

Koinonia is always the context of conversion, the fellowship in which lives are changed by Christ. No one is converted by himself; still less is one able to keep growing by himself. Koinonia requires personal participation and mutual sharing with others. This is possible in small groups . . . .

I have watched proportionately more lives genuinely converted in and through small groups meeting for prayer, Bible study, and the sharing of life than in the usual organizations and activities of the institutional church. Those who penetrate into the inner core of the life of a local church will sometimes find and know koinonia apart from such a small-group experience.

The great majority of people who are not "on the inside" will come into koinonia only in the small group. In such a group, those who are awakened in a time of grace will be confirmed in decision, encouraged to grow, and enabled to abide in discipline . . . .

Bible study, sharing of life, Communion, prayer — here are the ingredients which again and again are found to provide the context for koinonia. They could almost be described as the conditions for koinonia.

The implications of this for the modern church are clear. Conversion takes place in koinonia. Therefore, the church

[2]Brunner, p. 11.

must foster and sustain the conditions in which koinonia can be known.[3]

One of the most telling experiences of evangelism coming out of postwar England is the Coventry story. A new cathedral was being constructed to replace the bombed-out cathedral. The church leaders realized that the dedication of brick and mortar was not enough. God expected the dedication of human life! For two years, pastors and lay people met in small groups to prepare for the dedication. They experienced a contagious kind of love in community. Stephen Verney, who gave leadership to the movement, reflected upon the implications of the experience for evangelism when he said,

> Evangelism is the inevitable outpouring of love. If the fire of love is burning in a church, that church cannot help evangelizing, and if the fire is not burning, then all its evangelistic effort is not only useless, but I believe positively satanic. Like the Pharisees, we travel over land and sea to win one convert, but when we have won him we make him twice as fit for hell as we are ourselves. For instead of setting him free in the Fellowship of the Holy Spirit, where he may become gloriously himself, we imprison him in an unloving ecclesiastical system.[4]

The small group is also the driving force for new openness and change. Grace Ann Goodman's study of nine congregations in the midst of change shows clearly the effect of the small group.

> Besides mechanisms and programs, the process of change in every case seemed to include some concentration on working through small groups (rather than preaching, mass meetings, or attempts to build up size. New ideas, support for action, and action itself seem to evolve principally out of the interaction within small groups.) . . . Small groups seem to include in their agenda's action, study that supports it, and fellowship that grows from it in varying mixtures. The impression that emerges is that although the church may act on society best through

[3]Robert Raines, *New Life in the Church* (New York: Harper and Row, 1961), pp. 69-71.

[4]Stephen Verney, *Fire in Coventry* (Westwood, N. J.: Fleming H. Revell Co., 1964), p. 76.

large, politically impressive units, change is experienced by its members best through small groups.[5]

Base groups are not a means to another end — they themselves are life! They can incorporate into themselves the full marks of the church, which include mission, worship, nurture, and fellowship. Numerous base groups discover that they can engage in corporate ministry as well as experience personal growth. So many laymen try on their own to become a "minister," only to get clobbered! They feel puzzled, defeated, and lonely. Support by a group can make the difference, especially if the group discipline includes a time for reporting "how it went with me" as well as "what I (we) intend to do." One urban missioner trainer told me, "No matter how well we train and equip a person for ministry, unless we build in a support system, we know that he will not make it!"

The Church of the Savior in Washington, D.C., has sustained a variety of small-group lay ministries for more than a decade. The total church membership is small, but the program is significant because of the vigor of authentic, action groups. This vigor is the key to mission engagement. Service-oriented groups, when they are sustained by study, prayer, and fellowship, incorporate effectively the full marks of the church.

But many persons refuse to see the church as a community of God's people, and especially as an organism of base groups. For them, the heresy of individualism raises its ugly head. They see "the church" being relegated to secondary importance, becoming nothing more than a means to fostering one's private faith. This view has its roots in the nineteenth century, when revivals were crossbred with frontier-style rugged individualism to produce the "real" Christian who somehow made it with God alone. Self-disclosure of weakness and struggle was a "no-no." This individualism led to a false piety and a rank-ordering of people.

The individualistic orientation of religion led to the con-

[5]Grace Ann Goodman, *Rocking the Ark* (New York: Board of National Missions, 1968), p. 210.

struction of congregations on a collectivist base. Brunner calls it the substitution of an institution in the place of fellowship. Congregations felt they were growing if they could count increasing numbers on the roll. The same false standard of success, based on playing the numbers game, still plagues the church.

Feasibility studies suggest that under today's mounting economic pressures, only relatively large congregations are capable of supporting clergymen, buildings, and innovative programs. For example, the General Assembly of the Presbyterian Church in the U.S. set the minimum membership for an effective congregation at 250. Many church administrators feel that 500-600 is a more realistic minimum. Congregational mergers and clustering designs frequently are last-ditch attempts to save what is left of struggling churches.

Yet, the tragedy of it all is that we are still not getting at the root of the problem. Most congregations are collections of individuals who are caught up in a passive, nonparticipation syndrome and operate in response to an authoritarian leader. Members relate to one another superficially or impersonally, and both the congregation and the minister play roles. We could never understand Jesus' disciples by looking at them one at a time; it is when we look at their corporate and interpersonal relationships that they come into a clear focus.

I have been advocating getting the church *on* base. For a moment, however, let's look at the character of *off*-base churches.

Off-base congregations see themselves as a collection of individuals who may relate to the pastor and God but don't have to relate to each other. In this system, each person is tied by a string to the pastor — this in contrast to the cobweb picture of on-base churches. The pastor, then, carries most of the burden; both he and the people are haunted by loneliness.

Another off-base position is for the congregation to see itself as a collection of families. At the time of the Reformation, the church stood at the center of the village. The family was the producing economic unit of society, so the church built its life around families. The church in Ireland still reports membership by a count of families.

I would not want to diminish the importance of the family to the church or the church's role in strengthening the nuclear family, but we do need to recognize changes. The nuclear family is no longer the production unit of society. Work takes place outside the home. Working wives and young people scatter to a variety of jobs. The scattering of family members can be seen on any family calendar, and the church adds to the fragmenting by programming along sex, age, and peer lines.

I am convinced that strengthening the nuclear family is only part of the church's answer. I need and enjoy my family, but my family and I also need an extended family of uncle-types and cousin-types. The church can construct these extended-family base groups.

Although nine out of ten people live in a nuclear family, the remaining 10 percent do not, and family-oriented congregational programs leave them on the outside. Invitations say "come," but the "singles" don't feel welcome. Our population consists of 38 million unmarried persons (over 14 years of age), 5 million divorced persons, 2.9 million separated persons, and 11.7 million widowed adults. There are 19 million married couples without children, 6 million adults living outside family households, and 3 million female heads of households with 7 million children under 18 years of age. How do we expect to reach these persons? Base communities can provide a setting for these persons to relate to other persons and be valued in their own right.

The basic unit of the church was not meant to be a large collection of individuals or families, but rather a network of small groups living as intentional communities. When our congregations, judicatories, and denominations recover the concept of living cells as the building blocks of the church, the church will again be *on*-base.

The Strategy Is Now

Some will object to laying a new base for the church with small groups.

"How's it different from what we have long known as the 'small-group movement'?" they will ask. "We already have these groups."

Although small groups have been *utilized* as a church renewal scheme, they have rarely been *legitimized* as a full expression of the church. They have been conceived as an adjunct for the personal growth of the participants. They have been considered an "extra" in church programming, and they have served this role well. Meanwhile, the *"real"* church gathers in the *sanctuary* at eleven each Sunday. It's there, with "everybody" (except the sick, etc.) present, that the sacraments of baptism and the Lord's Supper are celebrated. We have been so oriented toward the *gathered* congregation that the small group is relegated to serving as a means to a larger end — that is, to stimulate active participation in the corporate congregation. In this role, the house church cannot become anything but a half-way house.

I observe many renewal-type, small sharing groups on the periphery of the church. Laymen taste life in them and warm to their participatory style, but these same laymen are not exactly sure how the groups fit into the total scheme of church life. Church officers say little about them. Pastors fear them, for they call for a leadership style and leadership skills which the pastor does not possess. The pastor feels inadequate and keeps hands off, and when the group either stagnates and dies or blows up, the pastor and other stalwarts breathe a sigh of relief and say, "I told you so."

One pastor who had been "burned" by a small group stated categorically, "Small groups in the church are always divisive."

My response to him was, "If that's the way you feel, they will be!"

Let's legitimate the base group! Let's bring it into the center of the congregation's life. Let's get our pastors and laymen retrained for new styles of leadership.

Small groups have proved their worth. Now is the time to think strategically, bringing to birth new, legitimatized base groups — and placing them into the *mainstream* of the life of the church where they deserve to be placed.

Christian community runs on two tracks, one rail being the base group and the other the larger corporate body. The larger corporate body serves its essential purpose. The mass gathering for celebration provides reinforcement to participating persons and a witness to the world. The small group is not proposed as a substitute for the gathered larger group; rather, the two go together.

Our error in congregationalism lies in our driving a middle course and missing both vital ends; thus, base community isn't established and weekly celebration isn't sustained. We need new forms in which both the house church *and* the cathedral function effectively. People need both the intimacy of the small group and the contagious spirit of the large crowd. (They may not, however, need the larger group experience weekly — six to twelve times a year may be enough.)

The first needful strategy relates to the congregation. New base groups can be initiated to bear the full marks of the church. Worship can happen in the base group as the partici- pants minister to each other. Groups which have celebrated the sacraments in a house church attest to the meaning of serving each other around the kitchen table. Intergenerational learning and nurture occur when adults *learn* from children as well as teach them. Koinonia fellowship takes place where openness and trust develop. Mission happens when the group plots its course of action, follows through, and then reports back.

(A variety of models of base groups are possible both inside and outside the congregation. We will describe such models in Chapter 5.)

Creating a new, house-church base for the congregation may mean adjusting traditional approaches to church programming. People's time is limited. They must be freed from "busy work" if they are to find the time to pursue significant group experi- ences. Such sacrosanct programs as the church school, women's work, men's activity, social clubs, numerous committees, and even the choir will need careful scrutiny!

Studies by Richard Myers of the Church Federation of Greater Indianapolis reveal that churches grow both in num- bers and in significance as the number of face-to-face groups increases. Following this line, a congregational strategy for "base" communities would focus on (1) increasing the numbers of small groups, and (2) increasing the capacity of the groups to exercise the full marks of the church.

The phenomenon of "group closure" deserves our attention. Participatory groups reach a level at which they cannot afford to take in more members. A saturation point has been reached. Once the group has developed its own history, outsiders would find it difficult to break in even if invited.

While conducting renewal conferences in churches of various sizes, I have noted one constant. Whether the given church has 500 members or 2,000, some 60 to 75 people will form the active leadership nucleus. This inner group comprises those for whom church membership means the most. Responsible church leadership will recognize and appreciate closure. Let fellowships remain small. Let the kingdom grow by multiplying the units rather than enlarging existing units.

The efficiency of a congregation can be measured by looking at the number and the effectiveness of its subgroups. The strength which congregations gain through base groups can be appreciated when measured against the standards of *kerygma* (gospel), *koinonia* (fellowship), and *diaconia* (service). (See Chapter 6 for functional models of base groups; see Appendix A for a measurement instrument.)

The second needful strategy for developing base groups is to create optional forms outside the congregation. Denominational leaders have seen the conventional congregation, with its building program and professional clergy, as the norm of Christian community. Leaders in denominational and judicatory planning can help to open doors and to legitimate optional forms of base community within the overall institution. The new forms may not be residentially based and may not have a building or full-time clergy services. Should participation in the "system" be denied such groups because they do not fit the present norm?

In Jacksonville, Florida, there's a communal group of forty persons which embodies the full marks of the church. Led by a Presbyterian clergyman, they worship, support each other, submit to work and discipline, evangelize, and engage in outside ministries. They are black and white, old and young, educated and unlettered. Using the standards enunciated by most denominations, this group illustrates "church alive." But how does the *establishment* relate to a Christian *commune*? The tendency is to draw back, but I ask: Why not recognize the commune as a form of the church and allow it full participation in judicatory events and decisions?

One hopeful product of the Consultation on Church Union (whether or not COCU ever results in church merger) is a parish plan in which house churches, communes, and task groups can function alongside, and in a supportive relationship with, residential congregations. Inclusion of diverse forms would open the system to fresh air. Lay participation would increase. Many base communities function with leadership from lay, worker-priest, or part-time clergy.

I propose that we keep the "underground church" above ground. A few years ago, the press highlighted multiple expressions of the underground church. The 1969 estimate was 2,000 to 3,000 groups. I had fantasies of people abandoning the mother ship and piling into the small-group launches. But where did the launches go? They either overturned in choppy waters or drifted out to sea! They are hard to find today. Without support, connection, and accountability, the underground church is doomed to a short life.

I insist that base communities must be connectional. They must be attached to other clusters or to a larger expression of the church. Spontaneous groups tend to avoid the issue of authority, becoming instead a sectarian law unto themselves. In some way, "subjection to the brothers" must be expressed. The unity of the church must be expressed in the midst of diversity. On the other hand, the establishment tends to avoid the issue of freedom and diversity, pushing instead for conformity and control. Issues of authority and freedom can find resolution if the "brothers" will risk dreaming big enough!

The task of reshaping the church by building a base church of small-group communities both within and outside the congregation may seem a fond dream, but it is not an impossibility. The tradition of the church affirms it. Outside pressures recommend it. Insights into group dynamics and group process call for it. People are hungry for it.

The church lacks a clear and firm strategy for building the new and authentic base for the church, yet it has the power if it has the will. Sure, there are forces which restrain. Power does not shift easily; leadership styles change reluctantly, and participants assume responsibility timidly.

But what is the alternative? To die a slow death? Survival impulses promote change! The Holy Spirit continues to build the church! We can participate in what the Spirit is doing!

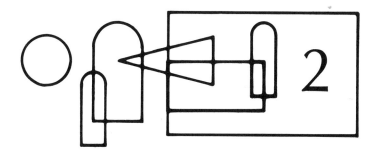

"BASE" IN CONTEXT

The base-church style which is proposed here as the vehicle for institutional renewal is not an innovation of twentieth-century group dynamics. The base church is rooted in history. Even as there is "nothing new under the sun," so the base-group style can be traced in tradition to Jesus and even earlier. It has erupted at various stages of church history. It is part of the Christian story. It is our own story!

The Biblical Context

The roots of base community reach into the Old Testament. The call of God to Abraham, the deliverance of the Children of Israel out of slavery, life in a promised land, grace and judgment — all these are examples of the *covenant* relationship. "I will be your God, and you shall be my people" is the basis of this relationship. Corporate identity under God's call and living under his grace and judgment provide the foundation for base community.

Jesus, in his own life and ministry, builds upon this understanding. His relationships with his disciples reveal a strategy which incorporated base community into the heart of his ministry.

Jesus began with a call. The call was: Follow, repent, deny, risk, work, love, and tell. The call went out to all. Some turned away; some gave excuses. But some followed. His disciples numbered many. He sent out the seventy. Women were included in their number. He did not begin with the twelve, but with a larger group. Then we see a clear strategy. From the many, he selected twelve. Luke says:

> At that time Jesus went up a hill to pray and spent the whole night there praying to God. When day came he called his disciples to him and chose twelve of them, whom he named apostles.
>
> Luke 6:12-13 (TEV)

The selection process was a careful one. Jesus identified those who were willing to leave behind other commitments and take a risk with him. He selected young and energetic men with a variety of temperaments, occupations, and outlooks. Each gospel account deliberately focuses on a new name: *"apostle."* Do the writers suggest an elevated, elitest group who were superior to the other followers? I think not. The apostles are simply identified as a core group which Jesus drew around him to send out. Mark records:

> They came to him and he chose twelve, whom he named apostles. 'I have chosen you to be with me,' he told them; 'I will also send you out' . . .
>
> Mark 3:13-14 (TEV)

"Stay with me" and "send you out" are the key words.

Jesus was able to teach, share himself, and equip his followers so effectively because they were small in number. He could not have done this with large crowds — not with a hundred disciples, even. The selection of the twelve as apostles was more than a selection of the fittest for an elevated office or position. It was a strategy to train a manageable number at great depth. Jesus' judgment is corroborated by recent discoveries in group dynamics which set the optimum number for a group (in which no one can either hide or dominate) at *twelve*! With the small, intimate group which Jesus appointed, honesty, doubt, fears, and hopes could be expressed freely.

In his charge to the twelve, Jesus suggests that their relationship with him will be as a family.

> Whoever loves his father or mother more than me is not worthy of me; whoever loves his son or daughter more than me is not worthy of me. Whoever does not take up his cross and follow in my steps is not worthy of me. Whoever tries to

> gain his own life will lose it; whoever loses his life for my sake
> will gain it.
>
> Matthew 10:37-39 (TEV)

The new family for the apostles is the intentional base community. Jesus cuts through the strongest of human bonds, even
family relationships, to convey a profound understanding of
what Christian community is all about. In the kingdom, one
will have new brothers and sisters. At the center is a new family
which will be a healing, supporting, and acting community.
Elton Trueblood observes:

> His chosen method was the formation of a redemptive society.
> He did not form an army, establish a headquarters or even
> write a book. All he did was to collect a few unpromising men,
> inspire them with a sense of his vocation and theirs and build
> their lives into an intense fellowship of affection, worship
> and work.[1]

The first tactic of Jesus' strategy was, in a sense, selfish. I
believe that Jesus had needs which could be supplied only by
an intimate family group. How often we picture him as the
God-man, as the Superstar who had it all (needing nothing from
people, needing only to give) and who fulfilled all his needs in
solitude with his Father. This picture robs Jesus of his humanity.
He suffered and hurt, was disappointed and angry. He also was
gratified. His relationships with the apostles provided a two-way
avenue for giving and receiving!

Jesus needed the apostles' reflections, love, and support. His
strong desire to share the last night with them in the upper
room over a private, carefully arranged meal must have been
motivated by more than a desire to get in one last teaching lick!
He was facing death. He didn't want to be alone. Later, in the
garden, he begged the apostles to stay awake and not to go to
sleep on him.

Yes, God could supply Jesus' every need, but one supply
channel was through other human beings. Jesus needed to live
in community. His leadership style, free of the typical "I can

[1] Elton Trueblood, *Alternative to Futility* (New York: Harper, 1948),
p. 29.

make it on my own, don't touch me," both gives and receives love in a context of base community.

The second insight into Jesus' strategy is to be found in his methods. With the twelve, he was able to teach in greater depth than he could have with a larger following.

> He told them (the crowd) as much as they could understand. He would not speak to them without using parables; but when he was alone with his disciples he would explain everything to them.
>
> Mark 4:33-34 (TEV)

Jesus' teaching was not limited to giving the "facts" — rather, he shared his life, including intense relational responses to daily events and the deepest feelings of his being. Jesus' method was action-reflection teaching at its best. He did not take the twelve away for a three-year, book-centered education; instead, he took them where people were poor, sick, oppressed, tormented. The apostles were to *tell* good news, but also to *be* good news. Real people and events became the context for training and teaching. The apostles followed a pattern of engaging, then withdrawing; working, then resting. In their reflections together, they continually referred to the tradition — how God had dealt with his people. But beyond this, they recognized that God was dealing with them in the intimate context of the base group. The base group was a crucible for experiencing and learning.

Jesus set the stage. He was absolutely honest in encounter relationships. No games, no playacting, no role-playing could survive in his presence. Furthermore, real feelings could be expressed and dealt with. Take, for instance, the very human feelings of fear, anxiety, anger, and pain.

Jesus expressed fear and anxiety. For example, he shared with the apostles the agonizing that he suffered during the excruciating night spent in the garden. Also, Jesus acknowledged the apostles' fear of storms and anxiety over a lack of bread and used these occasions to teach about a provident and caring God.

And what about anger? Do you suppose Jesus talked about "losing his cool" in the temple? Do you think the apostles avoided referring to Jesus' rage? I think the style of their life precluded such avoidance. Another example: Peter's outburst of anger over the humiliation of having Jesus wash his feet was faced and worked through, bringing a better understanding of servanthood.

Pain was no different. The disciples felt the pain of failure and inadequacy, and through it discovered and nurtured trust, care, and support.

Through experiences of pain and dismay, joy and victory, Jesus communicated who he was and who God was. The teaching of the masses on the hillsides does not give us the vivid pictures of God's ways that Jesus' relationships with the apostles do. We experience him through their feelings and relationships. Their hopes and fears are ours!

To test the apostles' learning, Jesus asked questions. "Who do men say that I am?" "Who do you say that I am?" Note the teaching method of testing impressions via feedback. While the crowds saw Jesus in Old Testament-related categories, the apostles (for whom Peter spoke) experienced him as "the Christ, the Son of the Living God!" The ways of God are best learned when operative in the lives of people who are engaged in intense and open community.

Note Jesus' response. "You are a rock, Peter, and on this rock I will build my church." (Matthew 16:18, TEV) The long-standing Roman Catholic-Protestant argument over this state-ment and its implications for the true base for the church obscures a valuable insight. The Catholic position overempha-sizes their institutional authority obtained through Peter. The Protestant position overemphasizes the creedal and doctrinal authority which comes through Peter's statement. Somewhere in the debate, the essence of Peter *the man* and the other apostles *as men* gets lost. The church was built by formerly weak, wandering persons whom Jesus made whole and whom he imbued with his spirit. Thus, Jesus was dealing seriously with *real people*. Could he have said, "Upon you, Peter, *and your kind* (upon you who have learned together in close fellowship the secret of God's love and ways), I will build my church"? I think so.

The keys to the kingdom become power for those who,

together, are committed to God's purposes. With Jesus, the disciples learned and acted. The power of the church lies with the base community of saints — those who have reached the depth of commitment and height of wholeness which make community possible.

The third aspect of Jesus' strategy to relate to this small group was one of building a model of "corporateness." He tried to put to rest the assertion that faith is a "private" affair; that the rugged individualist can make it on his own; that all one needs is the Bible and God.

God doesn't work in a vacuum. He uses the Bible; he also uses *his people*. In community, the person is not sublimated; instead, he becomes more aware of his personhood. Jesus establishes for the church the principle that people must live in relationships, and he epitomized the ideal style of relationship in his life with the twelve.

One of Jesus' prayers emphasizes the crucial nature of the corporate composition.

> I pray that they may all be one. Oh Father! May they be in us,
> just as you are in me and I am in you. May they be one, so
> that the world will believe that you sent me.
>
> John 17:21 (TEV)

Somehow, the mystical in-with-God relationship is connected to the apostles' unity, and this unity is connected to, and energizes, their witness. The gospel is proclaimed verbally, is acted out in deed, and is made credible by the relational life of the "brothers."

This unity and love in community become the marching orders for a dynamic New Testament church. After the resurrection, the scattered apostles were "put back together." Their new hope was grounded in resurrection faith and confidence. They were instructed to maintain close fellowship — to wait and pray *together*. The same pattern follows Pentecost, the birth of the church.

> All the believers continued together in close fellowship, and
> shared their belongings with one another. They would sell
> their property and possessions and distribute the money among

all, according to what each one needed. Every day they continued to meet as a group in the Temple, and they had their
meals together in their homes, eating the food with glad and
humble hearts, praising God, and enjoying the good will of all
the people. And every day the Lord added to their group those
who were being saved.

Acts 2:44-47 (TEV)

As the church moved out into the Roman world, it became
known not only for its preaching about a Jesus from Galilee,
but also for its style of life. "Behold," the world marveled, "how
these Christians love one another!" They met in small, face-to-
face groups. The church form of that day was the house church.
The New Testament repeatedly identifies various churches which
met in homes. (Romans 16:5, I Corinthians 16:19, Colossians
4:15, and Philemon 2) They evidently met in the larger homes
of the more wealthy Christians. "Households," which included
servants and perhaps close relatives, became the nucleus for the
gathered church. Church buildings were a later phenomenon.
The word "church" is used 190 times in the New Testament,
never with reference to a building. Not until the third century
(or perhaps the latter part of the second century, at the earliest)
were church buildings set apart for worship only.

The large assembly area in homes served well, affording
intimacy and closeness. The Christians greeted each other with
a "holy kiss." They gathered around a common fellowship meal,
where they broke bread in remembrance, confessed sins, shared
concerns and problems, reported what God was doing, read the
Scriptures, read letters from other Christians, prayed, and sang.
Paul suggested that they should "weep with those who weep"
and "rejoice with those who rejoice." Emotion was not avoided.
Only in the intimate context of the house group could such deep
relationships develop. Out of this corporate life of the church,
the gospel was powerfully proclaimed. Words such as "love,"
"grace," "forgiveness," "care," and "share" were part and parcel
of the members' human experience. They perpetuated the small,
base community which was at the heart of Jesus' ministry.

Because the gathering was small, there was no "audience" to

be reduced to passive participation under a dominant leader. Elder-pastors did assume certain leadership responsibilities, but ministry remained a corporate affair. Paul tells the Colossians to "teach and instruct each other" in the faith. Active participation was central to apostolic church life. The small fellowship was conducive for training and growth. The house church was not a token subunit of a larger, "real" congregation; it was a legitimate unit of the Church of Jesus Christ!

This unit was likened to a body, with Jesus as the head. The followers worshiped him. Yet, the body was diverse. Paul emphasized that each person was uniquely different. The Holy Spirit had bestowed a variety of gifts for a variety of functions. The leader did not have to possess all of the gifts. The communicants were exhorted to recognize the variety that existed within the community, to interrelate the various components in ministry, and to coordinate them in supportive love. This would insure an effective ministry.

The early followers' common commitment to Jesus Christ and their acceptance of diversity began to break down barriers. Through the indwelling Holy Spirit, the Christ who was in one person reached out to the Christ in the other. Master and slave, male and female, Jew and Greek, rich and poor — all recognized that they were one. The revolution was born in small, base communities — in societies of persons living out their life in Christ *together*!

The Historical Context

As we move from the New Testament context to the historical perspective, we see continuing in the early church those same community experiences and affirmations. One of the earliest of the creeds, the Apostles' Creed, includes in the section on the Holy Spirit the statement, "I believe in the communion of saints." This communion was shared not only with those who had passed on or were separated; it was also celebrated within the fellowship of living, geographically gathered believers.

We know little about any outstanding leaders and evangelists during this period, yet even in the face of persecution, the church grew. The evangelism and mission task was carried on by the communities which met in homes. They shared bread, worshiped, and hosted travelers and strangers. They did not have much power — they had been forced out of the synagogue. But their firm commitment to Jesus Christ and their understanding of the church as a living organism of brothers made this loose-knit collection of households a powerful missionary force.

Following the conversion of the Roman emperor Constantine, Christianity found legitimation, and the church no longer had to resort to clandestine activities. Now Christians were able to meet in larger groups in public buildings. The internal dynamics of the church changed. Bishops took on more rule. The church was organized into territorial subdivisions, patterned after the state. John Tanburn observes:

> Persons ceased to matter as such; the church was everything.
> Having passed through three centuries of violent persecution,
> just as it seemed to have arrived the church unchurched itself.
> As small groups where people mattered, the church had mani-
> fested a kind of love and fellowship that could heal troubled
> people; now it lost these marks of the kingdom of God, and
> showed instead those of an ordinary human power structure.
> They became the bridge from the Roman Empire to the
> medieval papacy.[2]

The first identifiable attempt to recover the original sense of Christian community was the monastic movement. With the fall of Rome and the chaotic times which followed, some hermit-types withdrew to the wilderness, and there a few disciples gathered around them. But the withdrawal of these individualists soon turned into an experiment in corporate living. The ideal of the New Testament Christian community superseded the ideal of asceticism.

In the East, the monastic style remained individualistic and did not become a creative and powerful force in society. In the West, however, corporateness was emphasized, and a productive system developed. T. Ralph Morton, in *The Household of Faith*, attributes the preservation of learning, development of agricul-

---

[2]John Tanburn, *Open House* (London: Falcon Books, 1970), p. 33.

ture, and missionary activity to the monastic orders.[3] Monastic support enabled many missionaries to go out — for example, the communities of Iona and Canterbury sparked the evangelization of all of Great Britain.

But the monasteries, too, fell victims to success. They grew in size and power, becoming structured institutions. Rigid institutionalism became an end in itself rather than a means to an end.

The seeds of base community were again sown in the Reformation, although fruition came later. At the time, other issues received priority.

The Reformation dealt first with the question of faith. The proclamation of justification by faith in Jesus Christ restored the foundation for creation of communities of believers. The questioning of authority in the church opened the Bible for the common people, who then could see for themselves the behavioral style of Jesus and the New Testament church. The Reformation asked: "What is the role of faith in Christ?" and "What is the church?"

Emil Brunner, in *The Misunderstanding of the Church*, suggests that the preoccupation of the Reformation church with the question of individual faith precluded the recapture of dynamic New Testament koinonia. He says that Calvin's emphasis on the invisible church, coming in sequence after justification by faith, is an inadequate view. Real faith in Jesus Christ is connected to the brotherhood, but Calvin's orientation to the church as institution blinded him from that insight. In the Reformation context, the doctrine of "the priesthood of all believers" was seen more as personal access to God than as a mutual, caring fellowship of priests who ministered to each other. Although the sect groups came closer to capturing the concept of "community," they got sidetracked by their search for a New Testament governmental order which could be adopted for their day.

[3]T. Ralph Morton, *The Household of Faith* (Glasgow: The Iona Community, 1951), p. 39f.

The fragmentation engendered by the Reformation has robbed the church of the opportunity to "put it all together." The Roman Catholic Church emphasized continuity and tradition; the Protestant churches emphasized faith and doctrine, and the Free churches emphasized community and spirit. All of these facets are important for a proper understanding of the church, but none must overshadow the rest.

One aspect of "community" life during the Reformation that we frequently overlook is the role of the family. T. Ralph Morton observes, "But the Reformation would never have been anything but an ecclesiastical movement if this new emergence of the family had not given it a new area of social living in which to develop."[4] The husband could read now (learning was no longer held captive by the clergy) and he began to take his place as the priest of the family. Faith was concerned with man's ordinary life, and this life centered in the family. Both Luther and Calvin reinforced the new picture of the Christian home. Reading the Bible, singing hymns, and saying prayers returned to the home. Instead of continuing to be a collection of individuals, the church now became a collection of families. The family had meanwhile become the basic production and consumption unit of society. Add the family's new religious dimension and we have a clue to the foundation of the "congregation" (congregation of families) as the emerging unit of Christian community. This concept still prevails.

Following the Reformation, revivals frequently broke out, accompanied by the experiencing of fellowship and faith in small, face-to-face groups. The most notable example is the Wesleyan revival of the eighteenth century. The social upheaval of the day, coupled with the insensitivity of the established church to the real needs of people, created a ripe climate for not only the warm, evangelical preaching of Wesley, but more especially for the organization of people into smaller units. Wesley's "societies" were subdivided into classes of twelve to fifteen persons meeting in homes, where the vitality of the

[4]Morton, p. 53

revival flourished. The focus of the societies was teaching, but they went much further. The members reported on the progress of their faith and they admonished and encouraged each other. They experienced the church as a community of believers. Furthermore, the formation of "bands" (groups of less than four persons) provided opportunity for confession, forgiveness, and deep sharing. Therapy, in an unconscious way, became a style of life. Ministry was mutual and shared. Participants became priests to each other.

Characteristic of the Methodist revival was the emerging role of lay leadership. Leadership was shared by the laymen in the "bands." It was located in identifiable lay persons in the classes. This indigenous, grass-roots leadership functioned in such a way that all participants claimed ownership of the group. The leader was no different than the others, although he did meet regularly with Wesley for instruction and further examination of life.

The societies provided a sense of belonging and stability in a time of relatively high social mobility. The situation was not unlike that of our own day, only it was less pronounced.

> In our own age, when change is the one constant, and when group ties are even harder to come by than in Wesley's day, the patterning of life around a fellowship group of a dozen makes very good sense. Indeed, many of the characteristics of the class meeting commend themselves to us with a new relevance today; sharing fellowship, the therapeutic concern, the lay leadership, the agreement to be present at the weekly sessions, the detailed inquiry into 'how things are going', the willingness of the group members to submit themselves to a group evaluation, and, above all the common loyalty to Jesus of Nazareth.[5]

In nineteenth-century Sweden, too, the evangelical revivals met informally in the homes, for the Lutheran State Church was not available to the evangelicals. Another attempt to recover the essence of New Testament community was the Oxford movement of the twentieth century in England, Switzerland,

---

[5]Robert Leslie, *Sharing Groups in the Church* (Nashville: Abingdon Press, 1970), p. 206.

and the United States. The movement fell into some disrepute because of its "confessions" and its orthodoxy in the practice of absolute honesty; it did, however, provide face-to-face groupings where people could attempt to learn Christ's love together.

A historical survey would not be complete without pointing to those many periods in which the church has been persecuted; where it has been out of step with the political power structure; where it has been forbidden to gather in large assemblies; where it has been driven underground, and forced to meet in small groups in homes and out-of-the-way places. One can think of persecutions by the Romans, Nazis, and Communists, and of countless efforts to stamp out Christianity on mission fields. Yet, in such times, the church seems to grow strong, recover its bearings, and break out and move. Why is this so?

I have often heard, "The church is strengthened and flourishes during times of persecution." I assumed that there is something inherent in persecution which gives muscle to the church; however, a closer look has given me new insight.

When persecution comes, the church is stripped of its security patterns of individualism and personal isolation. When dependency upon buildings and professional leadership is eliminated, passive participation is no longer an option. The remnant, who now gather in homes, experience a new set of dynamics. They must care for and support each other. They must search out God's Word for themselves. They discover who Jesus is and what he is about in the context of the "body." They are thrust into a personal experience of the corporate church. I believe that the essence of church is most clearly seen when "the heat is on." It is no accident then, that Dietrich Bonhoeffer's insightful book *Life Together* was written out of the experience of an underground seminary of "brothers" in Germany during World War II.

Today, reports continue to surface about the vitality of Christian groups in Eastern Europe, showing again the viability of the house-church form during times of persecution. The liberalizing influence in Czechoslovakia was traceable to conversations between Christian house groups and Communist leaders, including Dubchek and others.

The sweep of history affirms that when base-church groups form, whether by design or out of necessity, a vitality of spirit arises and enriches the church. At the same time, a common thread connects all the small groups to Jesus' strategy of the twelve, as well as to those early house-church Christians.

The Human Context

To understand the base group in context, one must also inquire into what really happens to people when they interrelate as human beings in community. People have needs, and either these needs are met in relationships or the people withdraw. The church proclaims a gospel of "good news" — a solution or remedy to the problems and needs which people bring. Yet, as long as the good news appears only in the form of *concepts* to be articulated and accepted, its capacity for touching needs is limited. But if the concepts can also be *experienced*, they can be *appropriated*.

Experiencing the good news in small-group relationships is a powerful medium for evangelism. The church was founded on incarnational theology — God entered into human flesh and acted in human flesh. Jesus invested his life in twelve men, challenging them to learn and grow by *experience*, then to reflect upon their experience, and finally to act out of what they had absorbed.

The Bible teaches that love of God and love of neighbor are mixed up together. Forgiveness at the altar is impossible until one is first reconciled with the offended brother. No man can say he loves God while hating his brother. Coming to know God seldom happens in a vacuum; it usually takes place within social interaction. God has chosen to work through his people — the church; therefore, we elevate the place and role of the church. We must take seriously the opportunity to communicate good news incarnationally within that dynamic fellowship.

Salvation is what the church is all about. "Salvation" means "wholeness" or "health," and it brings healing and well-being to people at the point of their deepest needs. It operates within the individual, bringing a fundamental unity; it also operates in relationships with others, extending to society as a whole.

The psychological sciences have suggested numerous schemes for outlining man's basic needs. Abraham Maslow begins his list with survival, then adds security, belonging, and esteem, and caps the pyramid with self-actualization. At Esalen, William Schutz developed the "Firo-B" test, which measures man's need to give and receive affection, inclusion, and control.

Here, we will focus on three areas of need — man's need to (1) *be*, (2) *belong*, and (3) *have* and *do* — and the ways in which the gospel can be applied to touch these needs.

1. The need to be

What does it mean to be an alive, whole, human being? What is an adequate picture of spiritual and emotional health? What does one who expresses truly human qualities look like?

By one's *be*-ing, we refer to that inner-life dynamic which is "in touch" with reality; which produces sensitivity, trust, and composure, and which reaches out to others. Personality and charisma come from deep within the person.

The whole person in his *be*-ing is one who, first of all, is aware of and claims his own uniqueness. No one looks just like me; no other person has my fingerprints; no one else has my personality. No one else has experienced life just the way I have. No one else has been influenced by the same persons who helped to shape me into the person I am.

I can look at my identity as a person in either of two ways: I can deny my uniqueness and regard myself as a "nobody." With this stance, I will live with feelings of regret, anger, and inadequacy. Or, I can accept myself. With this life posture, I can recognize my limitations, yet feel good about myself.

The second aspect of *be*-ing is built upon the first (awareness of one's uniqueness): awareness of being lovable. The person can accept himself and enter into relationships with feelings of being OK. The book by Thomas Harris, *"I'm OK, You're OK,"* did not become a number one best seller by accident. Even the catchy title touches people where they are. They desire to hear and feel that they are OK. To feel not-OK is to carry guilt and be fearful. If I am not lovable, I cannot trust the possibility of an authentic interpersonal relationship. I am blocked by my fear of rejection.

But when I can claim my uniqueness and feel lovable, I can move to the third aspect of *be*-ing — that of having value. A sense of worth affects a person's total orientation. He is no longer fragmented and weak, willing to be stamped on by others. Instead, he says, "I am somebody. You cannot turn your back on me as if I don't exist. I am a human being. You can kill my body, but you cannot take away from me the essence of who I am."

Feelings of "I am nobody; I am not OK; I am worthless" are expressions of "bad news" and unfulfilled human needs. But the gospel is "good news," capable of touching man's deepest needs. The Biblical witness says that we are created in the image of God. It says that there is no distinction between male and female, Jew and Gentile, slave and free; that God's love and grace frees us from all bondage, and that we can live as brothers in the family of God. Our life style shifts from fear to trust.

In the small group, acceptance is verified in the crucible of face-to-face encounter. The group helps the member to "tell his story." As he begins to present his history, he is afforded a context of love which suggests that he can be even more open. He can risk sharing his full range of human emotions — his fear, joy, anger, excitement, struggle, pain, hopes, and failures. He can even begin to articulate his doubts. When the group listens and accepts his feelings, he can claim his history as his own and begin to move from fear to trust.

When sensitivity groups and encounter groups first appeared on the American scene, they were vigorously opposed by anti-communist forces who suggested that the small-group movement was a communist scheme aimed at replacing individualism with "group think." Exactly the opposite was happening. Participants gained a new sense of self-understanding and identity.

I asked a Kansas City layman who had started over twenty small groups, "What is your secret?" His response was, "We have learned consciously to celebrate the uniqueness of each other." With that kind of affirmation, people no longer have to act in roles — they can be persons. When honesty, forgiveness, and affirmation function in the life of a group, it is little wonder that people refer to this life as a "religious experience." The group refutes the self-condescending protest of "If people really knew me, they couldn't love me."

2. The need to belong

Man is nourished by social interchange, and any forces which rob him of that "food" will eventually starve him out. Psychologist Earl Jubay says:

> We live on persons . . . We all have the basic need to exist in and on the company of persons, and without such fellowship, we die a death more painful than physical death. It is the death of the person. Strangely, the body may continue to exist for years after the death of the person, in which case that person is a breathing corpse. This is a terrible tragedy we see in the transients. Their persons died for lack of reaching for and being replenished by other persons . . . In a community of persons, one can feed his person. One may discover and fulfill his person in the dynamic meeting and creative dialogue which occurs in the genuine encounter with other persons.[6]

The belonging issue is greater than "inclusion" alone. To be "in" is one thing; to feel supported and cared for is another. Many groups have a formal reception for new members but subsequently function as if the newcomer were a nonentity! Recruitment for the sake of organizational "success" leaves the recruit feeling that he has been manipulated — really "taken in." In his gut, he feels "outside" rather than "inside."

The institutional church can be guilty of this very practice. Jesus had some harsh words for overzealous evangelists. Once the convert was institutionalized, he was "twice as fit for hell as before!" Instead of being freed in a loving fellowship, he was imprisoned in unloving bondage.

But the "good news" is inclusion at the point of one's need to belong. God's called-out people live in a covenant relationship. The church, Jesus says, is like people celebrating at a great banquet.

[6]Earl Jubay, *Search for Identity* (Grand Rapids, Mich.: Zondervan, 1967), p. 30.

A group of small children were tested to see what "celebration" meant to them. Each child was shown three pictures of birthday celebrations. One picture showed a single child seated with his parents at a gift-laden table. The second picture added some children but reduced the presents. The third picture showed a larger group of happy people, but without any presents. Asked which picture represented "celebration," most of the children selected the third!

Jesus' parables about feasts in the kingdom were "on target." Paul describes a community where people are to "bear one another's burdens."

The good news of belonging can be experienced in the base group even by those who bring with them an attitude of "I can make it on my own." The documentary "Journey Into Self" telescopes a sixteen-hour encounter group, led by Dr. Carl Rogers, into forty-five minutes of film. Early in the film, a "straight" intellectual professed, "I really don't need people." Later, when a pained girl next to him broke into tears, he sat by while someone from across the room moved in to comfort her. Still later, however, he confessed that he had wanted to reach out to the girl but couldn't. Then, filled with emotion, he said, "I really do need people." His self-sufficiency had insulated him, but the cost was agonizing loneliness. He found the cost prohibitive.

The move out of self-sufficiency and into relationship is at the heart of the covenant experience. We belong to God; therefore, we also belong to each other. God's love is free; we don't have to "earn" love by performing. The covenant is that we will love, bear, and be with each other. One can bring his sin, doubt, and variable feelings to a community and in return receive forgiveness, restoration, healing, and support. "I will be with you no matter what . . ." is the Christian response to the plea of "Let me belong!"

3. The need to have and do

To "be" and "belong" are not enough. Man must also have a sense of destiny and purpose, believing that life holds meanings which transcend his situation. God is at work in history.

To work, play, and aspire toward some larger purpose provides a sense of fulfillment. Industry is learning that once a person's basic security needs have been met, more salary is an ineffective incentive. Good relationships, appreciation, and meaningful accomplishments are valued higher than money.

For the base group, God's call to engagement, ministry, and service provides an incentive beyond self-perpetuation. Given this perspective, the group can deal with suffering, rejection, conflict, and failure. The ultimate transcends the here and now.

The late Don James of the Pittsburgh Experiment told of an ex-G.I. who remembered his World War II military service as the most fulfilling period of his life. His reasons: He was engaged in discipline. He lived in a context of camaraderie in which men died for each other. And he worked for a cause greater than himself. Intentional living — that is, living out of commitment to goals and purposes — is increasingly being viewed as a means to health. Intentional living is focal to man's need to *have* and *do*.

Robert Leslie, in *Sharing Groups in the Church*, isolates five key acts in the drama of "salvation." They are: (1) the call, (2) conviction, (3) grace, (4) crucifixion, (5) resurrection. He relates how these symbols can be experienced in small groups:

> It has always been the task of religion to deal with the dimension of depth in life. Religious language provides a symbolic way of talking about the mysteries of human existence. The symbols of the Christian faith provide this structure but for most contemporary people they are symbols that are neither understood nor appreciated. It has been the thesis of this chapter that the small, sharing group can provide an especially good laboratory for doing theology, for experiencing both the problems of life and the ways of thinking about them in Christian terminology. Thus incarnation, crucifixion, and resurrection, for example, are seen both as historic events in the life of Christ and as symbols articulating eternal truths in the life of man.[7]

The base church, then, is a place to which people bring the

[7]Leslie, p. 115.

same hang-ups and needs that they would bring to any other church experience. The difference is that in the small group, they can learn by *experiencing* the gospel in *relationships*. Sharing in a community of brothers who are learning Christ's love can make traditional theological concepts come alive.

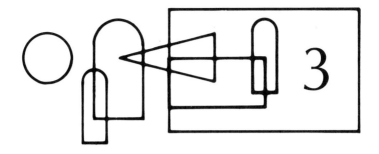

THE PUSH FROM
WITHOUT

The age-old argument for historians reads, "Does a man make the times, or do the times make the man?" Could the civil rights movement of the 60's have made it without Martin Luther King? Or, would the movement have taken place thirty years earlier if King had been born thirty years sooner? Perhaps this argument is as fruitless as the chicken-egg controversy, for it must remain a hypothetical exercise. We can, however, affirm that the times do set the stage for movements. Social, political, and economic conditions stimulate, accelerate, and ripen movements, including religious movements.

The Social Milieu

Today's social milieu pushes the church to find a new base in smaller, more intimate fellowship units. Voices from across the world cry for a base-church style. The base church is a very old idea whose time is now.

Let's look at some of those driving forces which push for change in the church.

1. Prosperity

Americans enjoy the highest standard of living in the world. We spend a lower proportion of our income on food and shelter than any generation before us or around us. Poverty still exists, but the majority of Americans enjoy basic economic security. People have time, energy, and money for pursuits beyond fulfilling their primary food, housing, and clothing needs. Their pursuits have led them down all kinds of roads, some of them

dead ends. People are asking about meaning and purpose, fulfillment and well-being.

Abraham Maslow's hierarchy of needs places survival and
security at the bottom of the pyramid.[1]

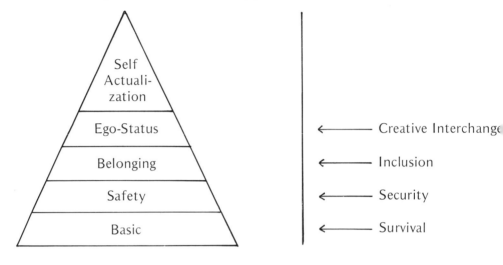

HIERARCHY OF NEEDS

Once the *"basic"* and *"safety"* needs have been met, people
push on for meaning through inclusion in community (*belonging*), through authentic interpersonal relationships (*ego-status*),
and through creative expressions and recognition (*self-actualization*). These last three elements empower and fulfill. The small,
face-to-face group relationship engages the individual in this
arena of life.

2. Mobility

I sat with a goal-writing committee for a newly forming congregation and heard one man say: "We are really a bunch of
'nomads.' I get transferred every few years, as do many in the
congregation. I think we should state goals which relate to the
care of nomadic members."

[1] A. H. Maslow, *Motivation and Personality*, 2nd ed. (New York: Harper
and Row, 1970).

Time reports:

> The average American moves fourteen times in his lifetime.
> One fifth of the population (40 million) change addresses
> each year.
>
> Many cities find 35% of the population moving every year.
>
> Six million Americans live in mobile homes.
>
> At any given time, half of the 18 to 22-year-olds in
> hundreds of towns live away from home.[2]

The effect of this movement on the populace is devastating.
Few families are spared. People are in a constant process of
finding new friends and seeking inclusion in new groups. When
they fail to meet their social needs, the result is loneliness,
alienation, and retreat into anonymity. In *A Nation of Strangers*,
Vance Packard documents both the mobility and its effect.
Time magazine's review summarizes:

> America has become . . . a nation of men and women who are
> rootless, isolated, indifferent to community problems, shallow
> in personal relationships and afflicted with "unconnectedness
> and a lonely coldness" . . . there seem to be increasing numbers
> of people who are indifferent to all close associates. Apparently
> they have what Harvard Sociologist George Homans calls a
> "lowered social capacity" – this may have ominous long-range
> implications. "Loss of group membership in one generation,"
> says Homans, "may make men less capable of group member-
> ship in the next. The cycle is vicious" . . . To break that cycle
> is the nation's most urgent task. America must "rediscover the
> natural human community" to which they feel they can
> belong.[3]

I would like to take up Packard's challenge. I pray that the
church will see what is at stake if the impersonal cycle continues. And I hope that the church will create new structures
which will move into the mobile streams to be the salt and
leaven of community. To build community among men under
God is the church's business. If the church does not move to

[2]"The Nomadic American," *Time* (September 11, 1972), p. 39.

[3]*Time*, p. 39.

break the cycle, what institution will? Certainly, a hedonistic, live-for-the-moment motivation will not create authentic community.

The church's recent pattern of moving two miles farther out to purchase ten acres for a new church taps only one mobility stream — the home owners moving into a particular geographical area. But nowadays people find community outside geographical considerations; they pick and choose friends along cultural, vocational, avocational, and educational lines.

How can the church reach beyond the residential stream? We know that church development is influenced by economics — people who purchase a suburban lot and build a home are more likely to buy property and construct a church than are the more mobile apartment residents, who are without their own turf. A property-oriented congregation is alien to their cultural style.

Experimental "floating congregations," which have no geographical footing, reach into high mobility areas where people are less likely to make long-term commitments and are more comfortable with easy-access, easy-exit groups which gather around special interests or concerns.

3. Density

Closely related to the mobility phenomenon is urbanization. People pack on top of people; they no longer know "everyone in town" — indeed, they rarely know their neighbors. This isn't all bad, however, for people do not have the emotional capacity to engage large numbers of people in intimate relationships. We necessarily maintain superficial relationships with some parties, going only deep enough to transact necessary business. Alvin Toffler calls this a modular relationship.

> Rather than entangling ourselves with the whole man, we plug into a module of his personality. Each personality can be imagined as a unique configuration of thousands of such modules. Thus no whole person is interchangeable with any other. But certain modules are. Since we are seeking only to buy a pair of shoes, and not the friendship, love or hate of the salesman, it is not necessary for us to tap into or engage with all the other modules that form his personality. Our relationship is safely limited.[4]

[4]Alvin Toffler, *Future Shock* (New York: Bantam Books, 1971), p. 97.

People need, however, to cultivate multiple acquaintances in order to sift out a close circle of friends. The circle does not grow very large, even in high-population areas. In a study, thirty-nine married, middle-class couples in Lincoln, Nebraska, were asked for a listing of close friends. Each couple listed an average of seven "friendship" units, a total of seven to fourteen persons.[5] Let's appropriate the message of this study: No matter how efficiently we organize large church programs and assemblies, people are capable of engaging in deep, trusting friendships with only a small group. Let's structure our church life accordingly; then, perhaps, we can touch in a significant way the lonely, alienated, anonymous nomads who pack together in our cities.

4. Participation

That this is a time of self-assertion is evidenced in the popularity of do-it-yourself activities. A new mood of "localism" provokes restlessness with decisions made in faraway places. Power consciousness among minority groups, community organization among the poor, and the multiplication of "rights" groups attest that people want to participate in a significant way in the decisions which affect their lives. Toffler suggests that "ad-hocracy" threatens to supplant bureaucracy in organizations.[6] Short-term, high-visibility, highly participatory, and even spontaneous endeavors appeal to people who are fed up with the inefficiency of monolithic institutions.

This restlessness nudges the church. Increasing numbers of special-interest groups form, including minority caucuses, political "fellowships," lay lobby groups, and evangelism program units. Many of these enterprises are outside or alongside denominations. Ad-hocracy says to the church, "Value us, hear our concern. Let us in on a piece of the action!" New forms of the church must be able to incorporate and utilize the participatory mood lest the mood turn into reaction against the church.

[5]Toffler, p. 120.

[6]Toffler, p. 125.

5. Rapid Change

The accelerated pace of change brought on by technology keeps our heads swimming. We have within our lifetime experienced more change than hundreds of years of previous history produced. Communication devices put information at our fingertips. For the first time, a war has been fought in our living rooms. My family did not have electricity on our farm until I was twelve years old, but think of the ways electricity has influenced my life since then.

Rapid change produces psychic shifts that are hard to fathom and manage. A natural outgrowth of this change has been the emergence of pluralism, which embraces different attitudes, values, and goals. Groupings form and vie against one another, producing conflict. Low levels of tolerance for diversity and an inability to deal with conflicting feelings paralyze society.

The world presses the church to embrace and demonstrate diversity in its own life — to resolve issues or learn to live with conflict without tearing the community to shreds. Toffler calls for "stability zones"[7] which can cushion and help people through future shock. Just as the medieval village banded people together for protection against the wilderness, so new intentional communities can become zones for emotional survival. Stability zones must be anchored to constants, and the church affords such a base. God is the Lord of history — past, present, and future!

6. Specialization

A highly complex society demands specialty knowledge and skills in order to achieve efficiency in production and management. Too often, however, the cost is stunted creativity and retarded personal growth.

A specialist-oriented society presses the church to act in two vital areas:

1. *Help the laity to discover and develop their full range of gifts for service in line with their dreams.* So often, educational patterns crush the creative fantasies of people, pushing them into dull conformity. The church must help laymen to break

[7]Toffler, p. 378.

out of their routines and dream their dreams. First, the church can provide a climate in which laymen can bring their hopes and aspirations to the surface, verbalize them, test them, and then either reject or affirm them. Second, the church can help laymen to express their dreams either through communication with other persons or through action, whichever is appropriate.

2. *Develop a broad range of task-oriented base groups which can focus their commitment upon specific issues.* Large congregations which adopt a strategy of aiming scatter-shot witness through laymen in their jobs and homes utilize only one mission tool. Base groups, on the other hand, can zero in on specific concerns such as housing, racial justice, employment, and the neglected aged. Specialty task groups can function with diversity in unity. But these groups will not just happen. The church must intentionally help people to find community, then assist communities as they engage in mission. Rarely do individuals maintain sustained ministries without nurture from a group.

The Countercultural Movement

Recent books by Charles Reich (*The Greening of America*) and Theodore Roszak (*The Making of a Counter Culture*) have stimulated a serious examination of the dynamics of the countercultural movement. Is a new consciousness actually emerging? If so, will it die out as fads do?

The countercultural movement centers on appropriating new values for society. Distinct and identifiable viewpoints vie for dominance; however, the tradition-laden side of our culture is very hard to unseat.

> The old culture, when forced to choose, tends to give preference to property rights over personal rights, technological requirements over human needs, competition over cooperation, violence over sexuality, concentration over distribution, the producer over the consumer, means over ends, secrecy over openness, social reforms over personal expression, striving over gratification, Oedipal love over communal love and so on. The new counterculture tends to reverse all of these priorities.[8]

The youth generation which espouses these new values finds

[8]Philip E. Slater, "Cultures in Collision," *Psychology Today* (July, 1970), p. 31.

ways to symbolize and communicate them. Their uniform becomes comfortable and inauspicious clothing. Long hair measures the reaction of the adult world. Music is the medium for communication.

Will the individual be recognized as a person, or categorized as dirty, lazy, and rebellious? Police, parents, and school officials find it difficult to look beyond their own value symbols to recognize and accept the other person.

Those who doubt the influence of the counterculture movement should wise up to its effects on the "straight" adult world. One example, men are having their hair styled. Many youth-promulgated values are being seriously considered in the mainstream of society.

The counterculture horizon is being pushed outward. Diane Kennedy Pike asserts, "We are already as a culture beyond the place of *counter* — in the sense of being up against culture — and into a real exploration of the alternatives. We are no longer just reacting against that other culture, but have now moved into pursuit of alternatives."[9]

Ed Courson, director of the Young Adult Institute in Dallas, Texas, points in the same direction. During the 60's, the institute developed multiple ministries to reach troubled youth. In the 70's, the institute changed its focus to middle-aged adults because societal pressures had moved up to the older age group.

The Church Without Walls in Kansas City found that establishment-type adults were in transition. They were reassessing their lives, including:

- a reassessment of values.
- a reassessment of what determines who they are (identity).
- a reassessment of their relationship to authority.
- a reassessment of how the past relates to the present.
- a reassessment of institutions, structure, and how decisions are made.
- a reassessment of the relative importance of intellect-verbalization and action-feeling.[10]

[9]Diane Kennedy Pike, "Beyond the Counter Culture," *Communication* (September, 1972), p. 28.

[10]"Church Without Walls — Some Positive Results," *Mission Agenda* (New York: UPUSA Board of National Missions, 1972), p. 4

Instead of espousing values which are uniquely Christian, American churches tend to reflect dominant cultural values — blind loyalty to country, success measured in dollars and numbers, organizational efficiency, social-class configuration, the work ethic, etc. The church frequently becomes the carrier of cultural values.

Ed Hutchinson reviews Margaret Mead's concepts of life styles — i.e., *postfigurative* style (passed from one generation to the next) and *prefigurative* style (developed without sanction by elders). He then translates Dr. Mead's concepts to the church scene.

> Without entering on a polemic concerning theology and religion, I would like to engage briefly in what I consider to be a theological analysis of life styles. If we conceptualize religion in much broader terms than the church as institution and understand it as realms of action and interaction, it becomes clear that life styles are just such realms. The postfigurative churches act in a realm which is closed to the future and narrow in the present. The new prefigurative life style provides a religious context which is open to the future and richly creative in the present. Both are legitimate *realms of actuality*, both legitimate religious arenas, but we have institutionally legitimated only the one style in most churches and the most dated at that.[11]

So, where in the church can new life styles find expression? The base church may become the structural vehicle for a religious expression of the counterculture. The base church can provide the context in which youth and adults can wrestle through and make transition into such new values and life styles as may prove worthy. Both personal and corporate change is, after all, the church's business. Values such as freedom, humanness, caring, and love are at the heart of the conversion and growth experiences.

If institutions are to be created around human needs, it is not too early to search for clues as to what man will be like in the future. I believe that clues can be found in the following dynamics of the countercultural movement.

[11]Ed Hutchinson, *The Cybernetic Regional Church* (The Bureau of Community Research, Berkeley, California), p. 9.

1. Nonrational

Tables are being turned on the traditional ways of knowing, and there is rebellion against accepted seats of wisdom and authority. My generation has taken the word from the top down, but new voices say, "Hold on! Knowing comes from within. Don't be afraid to trust your own feelings and intuitions instead of the institution's philosophies and regulations." The Viet Nam war pitted the "feeling in one's bones" against such a totally opposite governmental policy that disgust and disdain erupted. Students struck by the irrelevancy of some college courses have pressed for free universities and for a share in planning the curriculum.

In religious circles, the nonrational mood is revolutionizing worship. Myth and the mystical expressions abound. The Neo-Pentecostal movement has made giant strides in denominational ranks. Personal experience of the Holy Spirit locates authority within the *person* rather than in the *institution*. (This is one reason why the Quaker tradition plays such a large role in the Lay Renewal Movement.)

The Jesus People have by and large been unimpressed with church institutional forms. For them, "reality" does not depend upon the church. So now the church is called upon to find structures through which inner sources of authority can find expression. Much of our institutional insecurity grows out of the failure of the power/authority system to come to grips with other life styles.

2. Intimate

In secular society, people profess to make it on their own but are inwardly lonely. The hunger for intimacy expresses itself in a variety of experimental forms. More than one thousand communes exist in New York City alone. *Time* magazine's turn-of-the-decade issue forecast what the 70's would be like:

> . . . that more and more people probably will share the hippie's quest for new freedom, intimate social groups. The swinging-single apartment houses and the sedate, self-contained villages for the retired that flourished in the 60's may prove to be the models for other communal forms. There may be such things

as occupational communes, in which groups of doctors and lawyers will live together with their families, and different age groups may emulate the old in banding together in Yankee-style collectives. Individualism may continue to wane as men seek personal identity in group identity . . .[12]

One wonders whether the so-called "new sexual freedom" actually leads to greater sexual promiscuity, as many imagine, or whether there is simply more talk. Puritanical attitudes certainly hold less credence as personality and personhood are seen as vital parts of one's total sexuality. New attitudes release people to share in intimate group relationships.

3. Religious

The religious revival which accompanied the countercultural movement reveals the new trend toward mystical expressions even in the midst of secularism. The Jesus Movement developed unexpectedly. In 1960, few would have predicted that by 1970 most major magazines would feature the movement. Who could have foreseen "Jesus Christ, Superstar" or "Godspell"? The zeal of the Jesus People has upset many Christian homes and has baffled major denominations. The Jesus People lean in fundamentalistic, pietistic, and Pentecostal directions, rather than embracing the social-activist leanings of their parent churches. The impact of the Jesus People upon society — and especially upon the "straight element" — will be felt for many years to come.

The Christian tradition has not had a corner on religious expression. Astrology, numerology, and phrenology have become ways of life. Mystery cults look to the East for inspiration and solace. For many persons, transcendental meditation, Yoga, and Zen provide insight into the beauty of the human personality. Even certain aspects of the drug scene have religious overtones.

The world presses the church to rediscover those ancient arts

[12]"The Next Decade: A Search for Goals," *Time* (December 19, 1969), pp. 22-23. Reprinted with permission.

of prayer and meditation. Appreciation of the mystical dimensions of life challenges the validity of intellectualism and activism. If people do not find opportunities for mystical expressions within church structures, they will look outside.

4. Participatory

The countercultural movement reinforces the quest for participation and involvement. The student revolt in France in 1968 centered on the issue of greater participation in the institutions which affected the students' lives. The heavy involvement of young people on both sides of the 1972 American presidential election, coupled with the lowering of the voting age, reveals a new and vigorous political mood. The question for the church is: Will we provide activists with a constructive outlet for their feelings and energies, or will we, through default, fail to tap this vast reservoir?

5. Temporary

Our throw-away economic patterns surround us. Our indifferent handling of material things undermines our attitude toward people — they can also be judged obsolete and thus valueless to us.

We build a series of temporary relationships. The effect is felt in family life. Many couples decline to vow fidelity "till death do us part." Temporary marriages operate only so long as the two people are compatible; when individual growth or personality changes pull them in different directions, they terminate the contract.

Organizations also have difficulty recruiting members "for life." People commit themselves to specific, short-term endeavors; as these enterprises terminate, they move on to new pursuits. Again, society nudges the church. The church calls for life-long membership, and rightly so, for discipleship is lifelong. But cannot the church remain constant in nature while offering participation options? People on the move geographically, emotionally, and spiritually should be helped into and out of meaningful short-term communities. Many fifty-year-olds go through the same routines of church school and worship that they experienced in their twenties. And we wonder why they are bored!

The Human-Potential Movement

The human-potential movement could be considered within the context of the counterculture, but because of its formidable impact upon the church's agenda, it warrants separate consideration here. No single movement in contemporary history will reshape the church so radically as will the human-potential movement. It will affect Christian education, worship practices, and the planning process. It will generate new forms. It will challenge and test our theology.

The human-potential movement has strong influence because it is in the same business as the church — the *people* business. It asks the same basic questions: What does it mean to be human? How can people learn to live in community? How can people grow in wholeness? How can people create and enjoy beauty? How can people experience wonder, awe, and mystery? How can people live closer to their potential for love? These are *religious* questions! We should not be surprised to hear people who have participated in a human-relations event describe it as a religious experience. In the intimacy of an honest, caring group, one's religious agenda (which frequently is not dealt with in church) gets attention.

Frank Potter, director of Well Being, left the parish ministry to found an organization which would create intentional communities. He describes the intertwining of the religious and psychological disciplines.

> I myself find the work here as coordinator very deeply satisfying, because I am freed of roles in a way I never was when I was in parish ministry, and yet we are working with what, for an alternative growth community, is a very large number of people. We are free in this setup to talk about God or about Holiness, and we are free not to. I see growth happening which I can only call spiritual; and yet, it is all so intertwined. I find I am getting my own understandings of religion and my growth in religion at present through humanistic psychology. And I am getting my understandings of how behavioral science is

actually being carried out in practice . . . by observing most
religious institutions.[13]

The human-potential movement is more than a discipline in
group dynamics for it operates on certain given assumptions
about man. It is optimistic in stance. The hypotheses assert:

> 1) that the average healthy person functions at a fraction of
> his capacity; 2) that man's most exciting lifelong adventure is
> actualizing his potential; 3) that the group environment is one
> of the best settings in which to achieve growth; and 4) that
> personality growth can be achieved by anyone willing to invest
> himself in this process.[14]

These assumptions rub against the church's pessimism about
man. While we cannot swallow the assumptions without thinking, neither can we afford to reject them without consideration.
We must go back to the Bible to recapture some of the rich
meanings of salvation and *shalom*. The human-potential movement demands that we do our theology!

The human-potential movement had its genesis in Freud, who
opened consideration of the human personality to the world.
Subsequently, the interpersonal aspect was explored by the
psychoanalysts, who sought to relate more effectively to their
patients. During World War II, patients were grouped together
out of expediency and with surprisingly positive results, so that
following the war, the movement was off and running.

While these roots can be traced, the science of interpersonal
relationships is essentially a new discipline. More data has been
accumulated in the last twenty years than in the whole of all
previous time. Carl Rogers and others pioneered the development of T-Groups (sensitivity-training groups), which promptly
were utilized in industry and education. Established counseling
procedures were transferred into the group setting. By receiving
feedback on how he "came across," the participant gains a
greater awareness of self in relationship to others. The resulting

[13]Frank Potter, "The House Church as a Primary Carrier of the Human
Potential Movement," *Communication* (September, 1972), p. 16.

[14]Herbert A. Otto, "New Light on the Human Potential," *Saturday
Review* (December 20, 1969), p. 17.

self-understanding is intended to produce behavioral change — which may or may not happen. The movement has met with mixed reactions.

While group therapy continues to prove beneficial in treatment of the "sick" person, newly developed growth centers focus on the "healthy" person. The encounter group is the vehicle used. Normal, well-adjusted people aim to actualize their potential. Art Foster, a professor at Chicago Theological Seminary, suggests these approaches:

1. For an extended period, center on identity and growth.
2. Structure experiences in which people will talk about both the positive and negative events in their life.
3. Deprive participants of their role and status identity.
4. Give attention to here-and-now feelings and how they find expression.

Foster moves far beyond the T-Group, using a variety of structured "devices." He elaborates:

"I utilize a wide range of inventions — gestalt therapy, bio-energetic therapy, psychosynthesis, psychodrama, sensory awareness, nonverbal communication, meditation, personal journal writing, and yoga. At the same time I protect individuals from the manipulative pressure of the group whenever this becomes necessary, and I ask each person to decide for himself that in which he will or will not participate."[15]

One may find encounter groups in growth centers (60 to 70 exist), colleges, universities, and churches. The minimum time for an encounter enterprise is twenty hours.

Sensory awareness disciplines have implications for worship. Growth centers turn to practices which closely resemble religious ritual. Their use of dance, perfume, washing, and touch calls the church to consider its own heritage and to provide more total-participation ceremonies.

Closely related to, and in some sense a part of, the human-potential movement is the discipline of organizational development. Organizations can grow into health, as individuals do.

[15]Arthur L. Foster, "Use of Encounter Groups in the Church," *The Journal of Pastoral Care* (September, 1972), p. 149.

Some principles which are operative for individuals and small groups can be projected to organizations. Organizations can work toward open communication, clear goals, concrete decisions, conflict resolution, and problem-solving. Many organizational problems can be traced to interpersonal problems which jam the system. Skilled leadership is needed to unjam the blockage. Denominational structures are spending most of their training money to develop the organizational skills of executives and pastors. This has become the "in" thing and the darling of continuing education and training. As a volunteer organization without secular measurement devices, the church has to adapt the discipline to serve its peculiar needs, but the approach is effective — thanks again to the influence of the human-potential movement.

I do not suggest that the church buy every secular "pig in the poke" that comes from the human-potential movement. But the movement is here, and it is making its way into the church. At the same time, the church has something to offer the movement.

God works in many ways his wonders to perform. Let's learn where we can and reform where we will to make his church an instrument of realized potential in the world. We have the gospel and his power with which to do it!

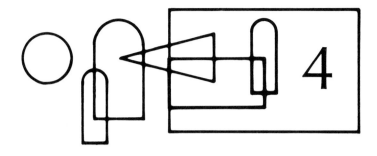

THE PUSH FROM
WITHIN

We have seen that the fermenting world puts pressure on the church. Meanwhile, the church stirs from within. Internal forces press for renewal and reconstruction.

Soothing, or Boring?

The bag is mixed. Some voices in the church call for change, but many persons are perfectly comfortable with things as they are — indeed, they may actively oppose change. How often renewalists fool themselves by assuming that the church will prosper once reforms have been instituted — for example, when the church becomes more relevant socially, more serious about discipleship, etc. The sobering fact is that those churches which are oriented toward mission-action, discipleship, or serious study do *not* grow — not in terms of numbers. The surest way to grow is to expect little from the people and provide a passive, soothing worship experience weekly.

So, mixed forces nudge the church. Some persons want security and call for things as they are. Others are bored with the sameness and want to move on. When we neglect hearing the restless contingent, we do so at our own peril, for they are people of commitment and vision who, in the pursuit of their visions, have in the past pushed the church to new horizons.

A group of active lay people in Houston, Texas, met together to consider forming several house churches to minister to some of the city's problems. Several pastors became uptight at the prospect of a competitive raiding party directed at their "best people." One who articulated the fear later admitted that he didn't think he would lose any of his own members, but the house churches might thwart his chances to recruit persons who had become dissatisfied in their present congregations. The group leader responded to the pastor, "The issue for these people is not *which* congregation, but *whether* to remain in a congregation or not."

Don Parkinson reported that of those persons who formed the Church Without Walls in Kansas City, more than one-half had already dropped out of church or were in the process of dropping out. Life styles change, and voluntary organizations which cannot change so that they continue to engage the energies and commitments of changed persons will lose out. Church rigidity and the inroads of secularization will force congregations already suffering from reduced membership and strained budgets to consider dissolution, merger, or a realignment of resources and structures.

Squeaky hinges in the church cry for oil. They find the program dull and lacking challenge. They are bored. Several root-causes lie behind the boredom.

I will never forget the shock of those first few worship services in which I "participated" after moving from the pastorate into denominational administration. As a worship leader, I had been fully involved in praying, preaching, and responding to the needs of others. But then I experienced what many laymen feel as they sit in the pew: I just sat there!

Later, I shared with a former elder/parishioner of mine the impact of the experience.

"I know how you feel," he said. "I have been feeling that way for five years!"

Those five years extended back into *my* ministry. We were close friends, but he hadn't described his restlessness to me for fear of hurting my feelings.

Ed Hutchinson observes:

> Participation is one of the primary theological categories of the new life styles. If I sit in a pew on Sunday and dream my way through the service, my realm of participation actuality

or religious experience is my dream and not the service. We have discovered that about 40% of the people who sit in pews every Sunday lack any sense of participation which would enable them to identify their religious life with the public worship being conducted by a minister.[1]

The one-way, from-the-top-down, authoritarian posture of the church affects its total life, including its teaching, worship, and ministry. It fosters a restlessness among the laity.

Irrelevance

How well does the church help people to shape values which can be translated into the secular world? Do the values of mass urban culture overshadow those which Christians affirm? One of Arizona's largest banks conducted research to identify the involvement of its employees in organizations and groups outside the bank and to discover the effect of these affiliations on the employee in his personal life, his work, and in the larger community. In 5,000 returned questionnaires, fewer than 200 persons listed the church as part of their outside life. (This in spite of the fact that church relationship is popularly regarded to be "good business"!) Of those who said they belonged to a church, most reported that it was important for their personal lives but had very little meaning in the community, and even less meaning in their jobs. And, mind you, people spend one-third of their time on the job.[2]

Size and Rigidity

Researchers say that a group of seven persons is the most efficient number for the effective transmission of information; that one person's maximum circle of close friends at any one time is seven to fourteen; that managers can effectively supervise

[1] Ed Hutchinson, *The Cybernetic Regional Church* (The Bureau of Community Research, Berkeley, California), pp. 9-10.

[2] "Worker-Priest: A Mission and Style of Ministry for the 70's," *An Exploration into Worker Ministries* (New York: Board of Homeland Ministries, The United Church of Christ, 1971), p. 2.

only seven to twenty employees, and that social action is most effective when it is the task of a small-group force. With these principles before me, I shudder to think what the church does to people by gathering them in large groups only. No wonder people hardly know each other!

While working with established congregations in planning for renewal conferences, I constantly hear members complain that they are strangers to each other. Yet, a short period of intimate sharing breaks barriers. After only one hour spent in a small, face-to-face group, one man said, "I have known old Charlie, here, in this church for ten years, but I really met him for the first time tonight." Large groups, even when they periodically engage in coffee-cup chatter, do not go deeply enough to build community.

Largeness of size and organizational efficiency patterns breed a rigidity which is hard to crack. For many, church involvement is a ladder-climbing game. One layman who had climbed to the top as chairman of the official board in a 3,500-member church looked back on the climb with feelings of frustration and anger. He discovered that community had not automatically happened on the way up.

When we first initiated the Lay Renewal Gathering program in the Presbyterian Church, I expected that the smaller churches would be the first to grab hold and that the larger churches would lag. To my surprise, the opposite happened. Tall-steepled "First Presbyterian" types took it first. The larger, more rigid, more monolithic and institutionalized the churches were, the more desperate they were to grab any straws that blew in the renewal winds. Forces within these churches were calling for smaller, more personal groupings and for more functional diversity.

Denominationalism

"It is no longer possible for Protestantism to survive in its present form," writes Stephen Rose. "The present denominational organization of the churches is obsolete."[3]

[3]Stephen C. Rose, *The Grass Roots Church* (New York: Holt, Rinehart and Winston, 1966), p. 3.

The readiness with which people switch denominations reflects a grass-roots ecumenism. Fear of ecumenical merger does not spring from people's concern over wiping away denominational distinctions so much as it rests upon an aversion to the creation of an even larger, more authoritarian, monolithic super-church. Members have "had it up to here" with denominational machinery and programs. They are tired of committees which are created to plan and implement programs cooked up somewhere else and which produce precious little for all their efforts. They are, moreover, increasingly less willing to try again.

One newly organizing church constructed all of its committees around the denominationally approved plan. But when the leaders worked on overall goals, they were frustrated to find that their committee structure did not match their goals, making implementation an unlikely prospect.

The Explosion of Small Groups

Boredom and restlessness goad the church to reform into cellular base groups, but there are other internal forces at work also. One is the small-group explosion. Small groups as such are not new to the contemporary church; they have long served the church in many useful ways.

Prayer groups serve many persons as a vehicle for intercession and petition. Neither private solitude nor public pastoral prayers can take the place of "two or three together" asking in his name. The prayer chain is an adaptation of the prayer group. A parish which I served created six chains. Special needs or concerns could be upheld by people on short notice. On occasion, the chains gathered to check signals, to do maintenance work, and to pray for each other. While engaging in intercession, the participants became bonded in community.

Recent Christian education programs have been designed for small-group, sharing settings rather than the lecture hall. Probing and testing information in a back-and-forth process enlivens and authenticates learning.

The "neighborhood" plan of subdividing the membership of a congregation into geographical districts was popular during the 50's and early 60's. In general, it was found wanting, although there were a few exceptions. Their purpose was located outside the group. They were a means to the larger end of promoting the church program, fostering two-way communication, watching for membership prospects, or administering the annual stewardship drive. Rarely did the neighborhood groups meet to develop a corporate, caring life; they were not expected to cultivate the full marks of the church. Those few neighborhood plans which succeeded were characterized by well-trained officer-leaders who formed ministering communities. These leaders were not satisfied with being "under-shepherds." The zone experience taught a valuable lesson. People neighbor on an *interest* basis rather than a *geographical* basis. More effective subgroup work takes place when there is a common need or interest.

Committees are the butt of many jokes, reflecting the discontent of participants. Too often, committees are formed or enlarged as devices for getting more people "involved" in church work. Some committees work effectively, but too many fail. People see little happening as a result of their many hours of deliberation. The Achilles heel of the committee system is projecting final actions outside the group. Committees plan programs for others to do, then try to interest and motivate the congregation to respond. I find more and more people resisting placement on church committees.

Active churchwomen usually participate in women's circles. These groups' study and mission action activities have made them the backbone of many churches. Many pastors feel that without a women's organization, the church program could never be carried out. Even so, I have a hunch that women's groups, as a uniform program, have had their day. They served the church well during the 50's and 60's, but the scene is changing. Many women work outside the home and cannot spare time for one more "extra." Women are being elected to mainline church offices and no longer need a parallel organization in order to wield power and influence. Families are beginning to resist being torn apart along age/sex lines — especially by the church. In the future, some base groups may be gatherings of women, but only as one option among many.

The training which pastors are receiving in human-relations events is paying off in the formation of personal growth and sharing groups. One pastor who got "freed up" in one of Reuel Howe's clergy labs soon instigated eight small groups in his congregation.

Training events and resource materials for both clergy and laity are available. Sharing groups rarely just happen; usually, they convene around a person or resource. Without good leadership and meaningful worship and action, the sharing group will "plateau" and turn stale. The house church is ideally suited for worship and action; therefore, it affords both vitality and holding power.

Pastors are using group therapy to handle increasing counseling loads. For example, a group of bereaved people may do more for each other than a counselor can do for them in a one-on-one setting.

Task forces are used increasingly for short-term, special focus work because they are efficient, pluralistic, and self-terminating.

Through small groups, many persons have tasted base community, and now they want more. Some want to make base community the guts of the church. Past experience joins current interest to push for a new base for the church.

The Lay Renewal Movement

Another formidable force for reshaping the church into smaller units can be found within and alongside the denominations in the Lay Renewal Movement. Some of its expressions are anticlergy in mood, but most of the movement is supportive of the clergy while asking for new definitions of roles. Laymen have awakened to realize there is one church and its worship and ministry belong to the whole "laos," the people of God.

Recent World Council of Churches' studies suggest that a new mood is emerging.

> We still speak and think as if the Church were made up of two
> different human species, the ordained and the lay, one divinely

mandated to be decision-makers and the other to be followers. The new theological understanding of the Church challenges this radically . . . . True, the world can never be the same again. Kraemer and his predecessors and successors, and Vatican II have seen to that. There is now something like an agreed theology (surely a new gain itself not open to cancellation) which establishes that the whole people of God are participant in the ongoing ministry of Christ directly, not simply by grace and favour of an intermediate order of ordained persons. The Holy Spirit provides diversified gifts which lead to varieties of ministry, some emergent and short-lived, some structured and ongoing, distributed among the membership. The work of proclamation, of mission, of pastoral care, of self-forgetful service belongs to the total calling of the Church: and this has released the members into exploration of new relationship to the world, new forms of community and worship, new venturing in sacrifice and service. The people of God have become a pilgrim people again. They are not defined simply as the communities they have been in history . . . but by the movement they are.[4]

Even the understanding of ecumenism changes. Institutionalists have defined ecumenism within the denominational boxes; they see ecumenism as cooperation between established structures. But now a multiplicity of new, spontaneous communities and movements without denominational ties identify themselves as ecumenical. They draw people from various backgrounds; they join in informal networks or renewal centers; they even hold hands with denominations or councils of churches. These groups insist that they are part of the world Christian community! The World Council of Churches has stretched its definition of ecumenism to embrace "all in each place." The council is searching out ways to maintain contact with the spontaneous expressions of the church.

A number of nonconnectional renewal organizations encourage, sponsor, or resource the formation of small groups both within and outside churches through seeds which are planted in renewal-oriented conferences.

The most notable nonconnectional organization is Faith at

[4]"Reinherit the Church!", *SE/15 Study Encounter* (Geneva: World Council of Churches, 1971), pp. 2, 3.

Work, with headquarters in Columbia, Maryland. Its roots reach into the life and ministry of Sam Shoemaker, former pastor of Calvary Episcopal Church in New York. Shoemaker had been influenced by the Oxford Movement, but parted company when it became Moral Rearmament. Dr. Sam insisted on a more Christ-centered approach, with emphasis on theological integrity. His leadership, the renewal conferences at Calvary Church, plus a newsletter — *The Evangel — A Magazine of Faith at Work* — led to the formation of Faith at Work as an organization. Faith at Work sponsors numerous regional conferences in which thousands of laymen join in small-group experiences and make their witness. Frequently, those who attend initiate small groups upon their return home.

Faith at Work magazine has become an outreach voice of the organization, with identity as a journal of Christian experience for the "emerging church." Bruce Larson, a Presbyterian minister and a spokesman for the organization, espouses "relational" theology, with emphasis on the kingdom of four right relationships — to self, significant others, God, and the world. Faith at Work's ability to combine warm, evangelical Christianity with human relations insights and lay-centered mission action has attracted many laymen who were not able to put these elements together in a polarized parish church.

A second influential lay organization is Yokefellows, founded by Quaker Elton Trueblood but enjoying broad ecumenical participation. Small Yokefellow groups form around a series of disciplines — prayer, study, regular attendance at meetings, etc. The strategy of Christian penetration as outlined in Trueblood's *Company of the Committed* provides the groups with their marching orders. Yokefellows on the West Coast have developed a small-group process which utilizes standard psychological testing, with results returned in a sealed envelope to each person. The person may, if he wishes, share the results with the group. This approach strongly emphasizes prayer therapy. Occasional conferences and retreats at scattered centers reinforce the Yokefellow program.

The Ecumenical Institute of Chicago maintains a thorough

and rigid pedagogical system for instructing laymen in contemporary theology and mission strategy. In addition to a variety of nonresident courses, institute houses have been established in major cities. Members live communally in extended-family fashion and share in intentional worship and work routines.

The Pittsburgh Experiment seeks to involve people in small groups across the face of that city. In luncheons, for instance, men are invited to try a thirty-day experiment of faith, praying daily and committing as much as they understand about themselves to as much as they understand about God. The Experiment has resulted in creative ministries to the unemployed and to ex-convicts.

The Institute of Church Renewal in Atlanta was founded to develop and support Lay Witness Missions in Methodist churches in the Southeast. Lay sharing and small-group activity is the primary mark of the missions. The Institute now enables Lay Witness Missions nationally and ecumenically, having sponsored more than 1,500 of them in local churches during the last two years. The Institute, directed by Ben Campbell Johnson, has expanded its programs to include development of growth and outreach resources for the church, as well as experimentation with new church forms.

Christian Laymen of Chicago, under the direction of Hal Edwards, helps laymen start small groups which foster personal growth and provide support for ministry.

One of the fastest growing lay movements is Neo-Pentecostalism. Adherents make no attempt to join Pentecostal churches, preferring to remain in their mainline denominational churches. The Full Gospel Businessmen's Fellowship International, a major carrier of the movement, sponsors testimony, prayer, and "praise" events fortnightly in major cities. The prime carrier, however, is the charismatic prayer group. Neo-Pentecostalism emphasizes the experiencing of Jesus as Lord and Savior, the baptism of the Holy Spirit, and free-form worship. The movement draws adherents from Pentecostal churches, mainline denominations, and the Roman Catholic Church. The general assemblies of both Presbyterian denominations recently approved, with "guidelines," an open stance toward the movement, even though it tends to bring severe tensions into congregations.

Young Life, Campus Crusade for Christ, and Inter Varsity engage in evangelism among youth and young adults, utilizing small prayer groups, study groups, and training groups within a context of ecumenical community.

The list could go on and on. I have listed only the major carriers of the Lay Renewal Movement.

Within denominations, various renewal and witness programs push in the same direction. The Lay Renewal Gatherings among Presbyterian churches, Lay Witness Missions among the Methodist, Disciples, and Reformed churches, and Faith Alive among Episcopal churches provide opportunities for laymen to share their faith and ministries, taste life in a small group, and be priests to each other.

The lay-renewalist Keith Millers of the 70's taste new wine and, in their thirst for more, beckon the church into ferment.

From COCU to Vatican II

The Consultation on Church Union (COCU) has, during its ten years, attempted to unite nine member-denominations into one church. The plan of union has been both cussed and discussed. Many say COCU is dead; some critics contend that COCU was a creature of the 60's, no longer applicable to the 70's, where cooperative and grass-roots ecumenism prevails. Others predict that COCU will make it. (The United Presbyterians have pulled out.)

The viability of COCU is not my concern here. My interest focuses on the base communities of the proposed COCU "parish plan." Implications of this plan will continue to influence the development of new forms in the church.

The plan projects the parish as the basic local unit of the church. The parish would consist of congregations, task groups, communes, house churches, and other new forms. Membership and accountability would be connected to the parish, with a two-to-one lay-clergy ratio on the parish council.

The people of the United Church will seek to minister to a
variety of "worlds" and needs by providing many new forms
of ministry . . . . . Specialized ministries, the development
through experimentation of new models for effective service,
and greater flexibility in our organizational structures are all
part of the response to this need. (Ch. VII.8)

The precise nature of many new forms cannot be known in
advance. We seek under God that the forms of ministry
developed in the past may be transformed and made new.
(Ch. VII.11)

(We) search for an organizational pattern that would encourage
flexibility within an orderly framework. (Ch. VIII.4)

The parish will consist of the communities of Christians
previously identified with one or more congregations of the
uniting churches. Its program . . . shall consist of those
traditional emphases essential to the mission of the church,
and new emphases to be developed in new forms under the
guidance of the Holy Spirit. From time to time the parish
will celebrate its common life in worship and sacrament.
(Ch. VIII.20)

Parish life and work shall be conducted through one or more
congregations and may be conducted through one or more
task groups. (Ch. VIII.26)

A task group is a community of Christians focusing the efforts
of action and prayer on specific ministries and projects.
(Ch. VIII.28)

The parish program may be conducted in several different
places as may be most expedient for mission and for providing
opportunities for the members to experience meaningful face
to face relationships. (Ch. VIII.31)[5]

Many renewalists patently reject COCU out of a fear that a
monster "super-church" with layers of bureaucracy would be
created. Because of this fear, they fail to see the variety of
open-ended house-church options which would be possible. The
proposed "establishment" would legitimate base communities,
which would function along the old Catholic "diocese" lines as
a network of interconnected cells.

Denominational merger may fail, but the idea of enlarged

[5]*A Plan of Union for the Church of Christ Uniting* (Princeton, N. J.:
The Executive Committee of COCU, 1970), pp. 39-60.

options for Christian community will not die. The idea has been laid squarely on both denominational and ecumenical doorsteps. Gabriel Fackre goes so far as to say:

> Denominations are destined to disappear. Local churches will have to face hard survival choices. The richness and variety of perspectives and gifts within the Christian community will persist, as well as the multifaceted needs of human beings. The facts of secularization and polarization surely press toward a church model of parsimony and pluralism. If COCU did not exist, we would have to invent it. But it does exist — as a plan and possibility. The next few years will tell whether possibility becomes reality, or whether COCU will have to be re-invented by another generation.[6]

The obsolescence of denominational structuring, coupled with emerging ecumenical clustering and cooperation, places a mandate upon transitional strategies for new forms in which life and community can be shared and through which the unity of the church can find expression. Finding that unity becomes the current task, whether it is to be found in COCU or under some other umbrella.

Vatican II, another dominant event of the 60's, also makes its presence felt in support of the base church. Fr. Larry Hein writes a stimulating *Parable of the Train*,[7] depicting the Roman Catholic Church as the train, with the Pope as the engineer. When John XXIII took control, the track ran out. He suddenly stopped the train and invited the conductor and assistants to come up and talk. They, along with passengers from other denominational trains, proceeded to follow footprints in the desert. The footprints were made by sandals!

The Roman Catholic Church has not been the same since Vatican II. New roles for both clergy and laity are being hammered out. The layman has a new place in the church. Worship styles are being revamped. In house churches and

[6]Gabriel Fackre, "Parsimony, Pluralism and the Parish," *Church Union at Midpoint*, edited by Paul Crow and William Boney (New York: Association Press, 1972), p. 61.

[7]Fr. Larry Hein, S. J., *The Parable of the Train* (Atlanta: Forum House, 1972).

underground groups, people are reading the Bible and praying together.

Bishop Alexander Zaleski of the Diocese of Lansing wrestled with the implications of Vatican II for his diocese. He recognized that the church superstructure had been built from the Vatican down through the diocese to the deanery to the parish. But below the parish, no standard structure was imposed; rather, structures were built according to the context needs of society. To fill the void, the bishop instituted "neighborhood communions." His message to the church, *Agony and Ectasy in Building a Christian Community*, was presented with the following comments:

> From our most ancient Apostolic Creed, we believe in the Holy Catholic Church as a communion of saints in which communion there is forgiveness of sins and a beginning already of resurrection and life everlasting.
>
> The Vatican Council reflects upon this Apostolic Community of faith and love revealed by Jesus Christ in its *Dogmatic Constitution on the Church*, 'For all of us, who are sons of God and constitute one family in Christ, as long as we remain in communion with one another in mutual charity and in one praise of the most Holy Trinity, are corresponding with the intimate vocation of the Church and partaking in foretaste the liturgy of consummate glory.'
>
> As your Bishop, I share this same communion of loving faith with you and my brother Bishops throughout the world. It is my hope that through the step of neighborhood communion, we may give greater witness to Jesus . . . .[8]

Bishop Zaleski grouped approximately ten families into each neighborhood communion for fellowship and worship.

Other Catholic experiments of "floating congregations" are putting the household structure to work.

While the Protestant churches have continued to embrace uniformity, the Roman Catholic Church has moved to encompass diversity. Special orders have been created around concerns and emphases. A parish may have a geographical *or* a national

[8]Bishop Alexander Zaleski, *Agony and Ecstasy in Building a Christian Community* (unpublished pamphlet).

context boundary. (For instance, a parish may be composed of a scattered nationality group.) Our quest for new structures can be richly informed by Catholic patterns, both antedating and postdating Vatican II.

Internal pressures are hastening the day when church structure will be based on a network of diverse, living, small-group units. In the next chapter, we will look at some of the forms that these base groups can take.

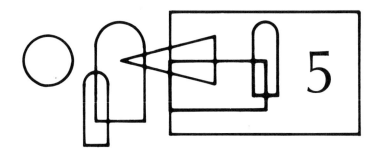

MODELS OF NEW AND ALTERNATE FORMS

The external and internal forces which we have identified press for renewal in the church. People taste new wine — they discover a new mood and spirit in the church. But in order to deal adequately with the totality of renewal issues, attention must also be given to the wineskins. Jesus cautioned against putting new wine into old and brittle wineskins. New wine calls for new wineskins.

So, now we want to get specific. We want to identify models of new church forms which can contain the new life of intimate group experience. Far more options exist than one might imagine.

Without equivocation, I want to affirm a connectional position. Base-church groups must function in relationship with the established church structures. Our task is to find ways in which the connection can be maintained.

The connection must allow the base groups considerable freedom to express their own life dynamic; they must not be smothered by the larger institution. Dialogue can provide the "establishment" with insights into spontaneous group life while providing the base churches with insights of the church's rich tradition. The connection must express the unity of the whole church while cultivating varieties of function and form. Pliable wineskins are urgently needed both within congregational life and outside it.

The best way to explore the various options for connecting base-church groups to the "system" is to chart them in diagrams.

I will suggest seven. They are only suggestive, not exhaustive, for many variations and combinations are possible. I will describe each model's configuration, giving examples; evaluate each model, and suggest ways to initiate it.

1. The Overlay Base Church

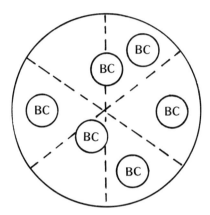

The *overlay base church* functions within a congregation which continues to carry a traditional church program. Regular church-school sessions and congregational worship are held (usually on Sunday morning). Church programming usually focuses on well-identified organizations of women of the church, men of the church, and youth groups, along with special events to which the whole congregation is invited.

In *addition* to this conventional programming, small base groups are established. Participants share in regular activities of the church. The most typical groups are the couples' group, prayer group, study group, and sharing group. The overlay base groups provide an opportunity for some persons either to go deeper in their faith experience or to carry out specific mission tasks which the congregation as a whole is unwilling to undertake.

Various group patterns dot our congregations. Some are spontaneous; others are planned and guided by the official leadership of the church. Some groups are clearly accountable to the church leadership, while "mavericks" function at the outer fringe. Groups may be healthy or sick, creative or deadly, outgoing or ingrown.

The distinguishing mark of the overlay model is that little if any traditional programming is forfeited. The group participants go the second mile, beyond their busy church activities. They have not been freed by the structure to give their all to the group.

Examples of this model are manifold. Countless churches are concerned about people whose relationships within the church are casual or superficial. The base groups provide intimacy, care, and support. They can be seen as either an environment for personal growth or a base of support for mission, or both.

Recent examinations of congregational life reveal polarity; therefore, one key to developing effective churches is to enhance their ability to embrace and capitalize upon diversity in program planning. Support groups can be formed around specific mission concerns, such as peace, racial reconciliation, visitation evangelism, ecology, consumer protection, etc. While the whole congregation will not become excited over every issue, a sufficient number of enthusiasts will surface. Many laymen who formerly felt powerless and outnumbered will be enabled to engage in creative ministry with the blessing and push of the church.

The weakness of the overlay model is its competition with regular activities which loyal churchmen "ought" to support. One pastor told me, "We don't have much trouble initiating new programs in this church, but we sure do have trouble killing off the old ones." As a result of the competition, energies are dissipated and jobs go half done, producing feelings of guilt and frustration.

Another weakness of the overlay model is the tendency toward a "split-level church." The base groups are seen as elitest cadres, whether they tend to be pietistic or activist. Appealing to those who are "for real" to go the extra mile leaves those who didn't respond open to feelings of guilt and inadequacy. Some who do respond move to a station of smug pride.

The corrective is strong leadership exercised by the pastor and official board. Good leadership can help groups of various styles to get started and can assist them as they formulate a well-understood covenant. Groups can be incorporated into a flexible church program, freeing the participants to engage in "legitimate" rather than "bastard" groups. Leaders can be trained in small-group dynamics, utilizing the many good resources available. A pastor can find ways to include base-group experiences and concerns in the regular worship services, providing content for intercession, thanksgiving, and requests for assistance. Church leadership can help base groups to see and respond to wider needs for ministry and service.

Renewing the life of the congregation through overlay base groups should not be seen as a cure-all. Groups are born, and in time they die. The task must be worked at continually if vital groups are to form, grow, and reproduce.

Imagine how Church "X" would look if it maintained regular worship and education patterns, but kept additional routine to a minimum. The church could sponsor ten-week base groups during the fall, winter, and spring. People could elect to join groups on the basis of their individual concerns or needs. (Vocational transition, prayer disciplines, single parents, volunteer service, parent effectiveness, study, etc.) The base groups could take turns assisting in the planning and conducting of Sunday morning worship. At the conclusion of each base-group series, all groups could gather and celebrate what had happened — what God had done in and through them.

2. The Vehicular Base Church

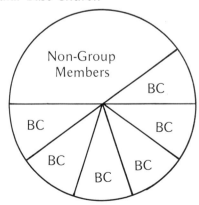

In the *vehicular base church*, the groups are called upon to carry the total freight of the congregation's program and ministry. Members are received into the congregation-at-large, then recruited into one of the several base groups. Not all the members respond to this invitation. If they don't, they can still share in the corporate worship experience and in church school study classes. And they would, of course, be able to receive pastoral counseling. But with the exceptions I've noted, there are no programs outside the base groups.

Each group incorporates the full marks of the church. Each group studies, fellowships, worships, and engages in a specific mission project.

The pastor and official board play a key role. Usually one representative from each base group sits on the official board to coordinate the work of the groups with the total church. Each group is accountable to the board for its actions and life, while the board provides support (including money) for mission projects.

The Trinity Presbyterian Church in Harrisonburg, Virginia, has constructed its life along "vehicular" lines. Eight years ago, this newly formed church decided not to build a church building; instead, it chose to continue to use a large former residence for Sunday corporate worship and church school. The primary church program was to be expressed in house churches. Each house church had a special mission — coffee house, prison, clothes closet, drama, retarded children, etc. The pastor, the Reverend Don Allen, describes their experience in *Barefoot in the Church*. The traditional Sunday morning programs were continued until recently, when the congregation decided to conduct Christian education and worship in the house churches the third Sunday of every month. This brought the children into an intergenerational house-church experience. One of the house churches meets in the church building on the third Sunday to include visitors and those persons who have elected not to join a base group.

The Three Chopt Presbyterian Church in Richmond, Virginia, is another new church which chose to develop its life in house churches. The groups are varied — some meet for study, some for personal growth, some for dialogue with other groups, and some for mission. The conventional Sunday morning programs are maintained, making this a variation of the vehicular plan. While each group does not carry the complete marks of the church, when the respective concerns are incorporated, the marks are fully expressed.

The strength of the vehicular model is that it places the mission task in the context of a growth and support group. Each group can develop its own life and mission, yet it remains connected to the total church. This arrangement provides the essential authority-accountability relationship.

New congregations can most easily initiate the vehicular style. Much work goes into recruiting people who are willing to "go in deep," and a new congregation is best able to pursue this kind of contract. Moving a traditional congregation from the overlay style to the vehicular style is difficult.

The transition requires much freeing and energizing. One congregation of 1,200 members laid the groundwork for two years before making the transition. Yet, with all this effort, only 150 members went into house groups. Perhaps a slow transition — freeing those who are ready and gradually cultivating new groups — is the most productive method.

3. The Para-Base Church

The *para-base church* consists of a small group of persons who, because of a specific concern, are drawn out of two or more congregations and across denominational lines, evidencing a kind of grass-roots ecumenism.

Examples are found in the Neo-Pentecostal "spiritual growth" movement, where the emphasis is on experiencing the Holy Spirit and appropriating his gifts in the context of praise and celebration. Often, Roman Catholics and Protestants band together in the fellowship groups.

The congregations out of which people are drawn for para-base groups exercise little or no control over the groups, even though the participants continue to be members.

Para-base groups may come together over a concern or issue in society. The leadership of a cluster of congregations (either of one denomination or an ecumenical mix) can convene the social action groups.

"Project Understanding," a research effort among churches in Southern California, attempted to bring about social change in white suburban congregations. They formed ecumenical support teams drawing the members out of various congregations.

> We found that tensions arising over the prospect of social change often provide impetus for a new kind of ecumenicity which may be one of the factors in the growth of underground churches. In our project we sought to institutionalize it as support for social action groups across denominational lines. Our effect succeeded in six ecumenical clusters and four single churches. Hence, while pressure on social issues was indeed schismatic in local congregations, it was also ecumenical in the sense that it prompted likeminded groups to form around specific issues. We believe therefore that, if a strategy for legitimizing such groups is successful, the churches can become much more effective in relating themselves to their members' concerns. At the same time, they can embrace those whose religious needs are more adequately met by a ministry of worship and healing.[1]

The Experimental Church in Winston-Salem, North Carolina, is an attempt by the Winston-Salem Presbytery to engage Presbyterians from various congregations in urban ministry. Through the leadership of a full-time clergyman, twenty-five persons have come together for social service. Their weekly

[1] Joseph C. Hough, Jr., "The Church Alive and Changing," *Christian Century* (January 5, 1972).

meetings vary in content to include Biblical-theological study; deliberation over books, papers, or events; interviews with "resource" people; project planning, and worship. The primary areas of service have been preschool education, youth ministry, and low-income housing.

The para-base church provides a supportive climate for persons who have special concerns with which the local establishment may or may not be in sympathy. The para-base group prevents able churchmen from either dropping out or going underground. This system may point the way for further church experimentation in creative model building.

A para-base church can best be established by a cluster of churches which deliberately identify issues in the community. They can then proceed to the second step, inventorying members of the respective congregations regarding their concerns, abilities, and willingness to join an action group. Establishing the base group follows.

A New Forms project in the San Francisco area has developed a simple device for identifying the concerns upon which people wish to act. People are asked to sort through a stack of cards on which are listed various concerns. They select some and eliminate others on the basis of their: (1) recognizing a need for change, (2) willingness to work for change, and (3) awareness of options. Results are fed into a computer, producing a quick reference profile of potential task-group participants. Then the screened volunteers are invited to come together to organize for planning, support, action, and celebration.

4. The Satellite Base Church

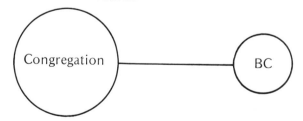

The *satellite base church* consists of gathered people who have a life and/or mission apart from a congregation, yet are accountable to the congregation. Some lines of communication and control exist. The satellite members do *not* participate in the program activities of the church, even corporate worship. Regular worship is part of the life of the satellite base church. On occasion, however, the base group may choose to meet with the general congregation.

The satellite base group may be either short-term or long-term, depending upon the understanding which the congregation and group have negotiated.

One example of a satellite base can be seen in the Druid Hills Presbyterian Church of Atlanta, Georgia. When Cubans began moving into the area, the church contacted them. The language barrier prohibited the Cuban group from sharing in the church's Sunday programs, so they developed parallel education and worship experiences, with the support and oversight of the Druid Hills Session.

Other possibilities can be found in Christian-oriented communes of young adults whose life style and dress are not "at home" in formal, "straight" worship services. Church connection provides communes with pastoral care and religious instruction. At the same time, the commune serves as an outreach arm for the church.

The Second United Presbyterian Church of Kansas City fell into a relationship with a living community of Jesus People. When the community's house would no longer hold the crowds of young people who came for Bible study, it was given permission to use the church sanctuary Sunday evenings for informal teaching and celebration. Soon adults from the church began to show up for the evening sessions; meanwhile, young people began visiting the traditional morning services. The church loosened up through this contact with "life," while the youth gained a new appreciation of the structure and tradition of the church.

The satellite model permits a congregation to experiment in a creative and possibly high-risk area without upsetting traditional patterns through which many people have found meaning and security. Its weakness is its liability for unclear or mixed expectations between the parties to the contract. Use of money, decision-making, corporate gatherings — these matters should be clearly understood.

How does one go about starting a satellite base church? Three options exist. One is for the local church to negotiate a relationship with an existing group. Begin conversations about mutual benefits and liabilities, then identify options for working together. Admittedly, this is a difficult task requiring trust and confidence. Many spontaneous groups distrust the Establishment. They haven't worked through their own feelings of rebellion, and they see their communities as "protest forms." The spontaneous groups feel that their life is validation enough, and that legitimacy via connectionalism is irrelevant. While the informal groups have to learn to deal with *authority*, the traditionalists have to learn to cope with *freedom*. It's tough, but the pay-off can be big!

A second option is for a congregation to release a group of its members to discover their own life. This model is similar to a method used by established congregations to start new churches — cadres are sent out to grow and to make it on their own. The satellite base church concept, on the other hand, does not envision growth and eventual severing of the parent relationship. Unless the congregation understands its own identity and has a clear picture of the satellite relationship, this option is fraught with all kinds of dangers!

The third option is to train and release either one person or a cadre of two to five persons to be the convening nucleus for a satellite. This requires support, encouragement, and training.

5. The Cluster Base Church

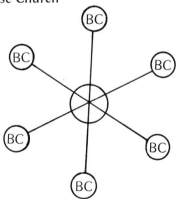

The unique feature of the *cluster base church* concept is the congregation's composition as a group of groups rather than a collection of individuals.

Most of the other systemic models begin with the membership of the congregation — the roll becomes the recruiting field for emerging groups. Some people can decline to participate, yet remain in the church. The cluster base church, however, does not provide a hiding place. Membership in the congregation is available only through participation in a base-church group.

The congregation consists of from three to twelve base groups. Each group attempts to incorporate the full marks of the church, including weekly worship (at a time selected by the group), the sacraments, education, training, fellowship, and mission action. Each group has one or two lay leaders who sit on the congregation's official board, where they coordinate the plans of the base churches, administer the budget, and engage in churchwide planning. The minister may make his skills available to the base groups, but he is not the leader of each one. He and lay officers represent the congregation at meetings of a higher judicatory, thereby insuring participation by the groups in the larger Christian community.

Cluster base congregations generally do not own a church building; instead, the groups meet in homes. The total congregation gathers every four to eight weeks for a festival day in a borrowed church, a park, or a rented facility. There they report their experiences and celebrate what is (or isn't) happening. Extended training or particular age/peer group functions can also be scheduled for this extended gathering.

The United Presbyterian Church of Reconciliation of Cleveland, Ohio, was a "floating congregation" cluster. Each group developed its life around a special mission task. Another example can be found in Christ Church, Burlington, Vermont. In 1961, this church decided not to build. In 1965, the congregation declared:

> Mission groups are Christ Church-Presbyterian. We have only
> to grant them the freedom authentically to carry out the

liturgical functions of service, worship, and study. In order that they may be so freed, we propose that the Sunday exercises presently practiced be abandoned.[2]

Worship and study were incorporated into the mission groups, and a festival day was scheduled for the first Sunday of each month.

Festival Day progresses from Scripture and sermon to inter-generational activity groups to a picnic lunch which includes the breaking of homemade bread and the distribution of homemade wine in celebration of the Lord's Supper, and ends with a discussion of concerns and strategies.

It has much the flavor of a family reunion, with the focus clearly not on the occasion itself but on the lives and activities, satisfactions and frustrations, and plans and goals of those who gather together.[3]

The strengths of the cluster base model are manifold.

1. It provides a streamlined and efficient management system. Communication lines are direct. Planning and decision-making are close to the grass roots, with firm accountability built in.

2. Good stewardship of time and money is exercised. The absence of building maintenance and "extra" meetings insures this.

3. Each group can develop the full marks of the church.

4. It combines the "cathedral" experience with the small, base-church experience, serving both the intimate, extended-family needs and the mass ("crowd") needs of people.

5. It provides opportunity for pluralism. Each base group will be unique. One might be a living commune, while others would gather around various needs or opportunities. Just imagine celebrations of this pluralism on Festival Day!

6. It goes beyond geographical parish boundaries. It can draw from a wider economic, ethnic, and racial spectrum than can most residential parishes.

The chief weakness of the cluster base lies in its demand for

[2]Edgar R. Trexler, *Ways to Wake Up Your Church* (Philadelphia: Fortress Press, 1969), p. 64.

[3]Trexler, p. 66.

strong lay leadership, which may not be immediately available. Another restraint is an ingrown need or demand in people for "a place." (We will deal with this restraint in a later chapter.)

A cluster base church can be launched as a new church with the cluster style built into the mission design. Existing churches with investments in buildings and with clergy and program orientations can hardly be expected to make the switch — they would rather fight! Also, persons who have not emotionally bought into the cluster style would not feel at home.

The clergyman who organizes this congregation should have skills for enabling and supporting lay leaders. Initially, most of his time and energy would be directed here. Ex-pastors who still have a commitment to the institution but are no longer in parish ministries constitute a vast resource of potential base-church leaders.

Growth takes place by multiplying the number of groups, each group forming around key leaders. Cultivation of the base churches would require the fine art of dissolving, changing, or rearranging groups, as well as initiating new ones.

6. The Solo Base Church

The *solo base church* is simply a small group which stands on its own feet as a church, without connection to a larger congregation. It may be organized and recognized as a participating church in a denomination or council, or it may stand alone, apart from any group and without affiliation (even underground).

The functions vary greatly, but most solo base churches which are organized by a parent church exist for the expression of a particular mission. Studies of these "style-centered" churches by the United Presbyterian Board of National Missions reveal that their memberships plateau quickly, usually in the thirty to sixty range.

The Church Without Walls in Kansas City represents this model. The pastor, Don Parkinson, writes:

> . . . the theory which lay behind the development of the congregation in the way in which I sought to develop it was: Talking about the Gospel and studying the Gospel and sitting in church haven't produced the results in mission and living out the Gospel that any of us are satisfied with. The Church seems to be caught in a web of words. Let's start at the other end — engage in mission; that is, in the act of doing what Christian mission needs to be doing. Let's organize a congregation with the kind of openness and involvement that you would expect in the church that is committed to the kind of life and ministry as it was incarnate in Jesus Christ. If words cannot carry the freight of the Christian Gospel, let's start with the action and persons will want to and be driven to become aware of and grow in the understanding of the Gospel of Jesus Christ. One of the major things I have learned is that that doesn't work either. The only thing left is to start from both ends at the same time. This has to come.[4]

The limitations of the solo group are obvious:

1. The small size and consequent financial limitations restrict the availability of pastoral leadership unless the cost is subsidized.

2. The intimate group has limited growth possibilities; it would have to change its style if it chose to accommodate more members.

3. The lack of firsthand exposure to other groups encourages isolation.

4. Experimentation to establish a new tradition is costly, time-consuming, and painful.

Solo groups tend to seek out like-minded "babes." Often,

[4]Donald M. Parkinson, *The Church Without Walls — Some Positive Results* (unpublished pamphlet), May, 1972.

they participate in informal information networks or connect through special conferences.

The renewal centers of Europe reveal an interesting support pattern. The Taizé Community in France, for instance, hosts thousands of young people from over Europe. When they return home, they form spontaneous "cell" groups for prayer, sharing, and service. The cells are ecumenical and have little contact with the official church. They do talk to other cells and the members occasionally return to Taizé for continuing support. Their connection to the total church is through the Taizé Community's tie to the World Council of Churches.

Starting a "connectional" solo church takes the firm support of a church judicatory which is willing to experiment. The Reverend Bob Ross felt that kind of support from his bishop in Birmingham, Alabama, while founding Incarnation Church. The payoff was eventually seen in the diocese, where members of the church are now actively involved in program and mission committees.

One more word of caution. Many solo groups have leaders and participants who are on the rebound from the institutional church. If they have left in negative reaction to what was or was not happening, they may be motivated out of a "we'll show them" attitude, and this will cause problems. A style-centered solo base church may not initially be able to deal with the extra agenda of anger and guilt!

7. The Chain Base Church

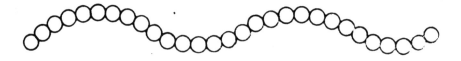

The *chain base church* represents a connectional system in which each base group intentionally relates to at least two other base groups. The areas of common activity vary. Some groups simply exchange information through their leaders; others arrange one or more experiences in which the groups share in worship, fellowship, or ministry.

A network of groups in Minneapolis (the Agora community) meets corporately on the fourth Sunday, while the groups "pair off" each second Sunday. The community has constructed a combination of the cluster and the chain models.

The chain system affords opportunities for sharing, thus discouraging isolation. Its weakness lies in tenuous linkage. Unless the leaders execute a contract, the chain could fall apart. Servicing and leadership by a "parent" body would be nearly impossible.

One manageable option might be the following configuration:

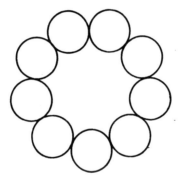

However, to keep the links connected by designed common experience would require a resourceful leader.

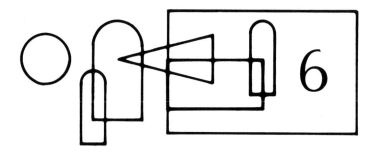

FUNCTIONAL MODELS OF BASE COMMUNITY

Just what is a small group? How does it work? What do you do? How do you behave? Anyone who has participated in a small group knows that it is difficult to explain to an uninitiated inquirer what it is and what happens. It's like trying to describe your first kiss!

Base groups are difficult to describe; their variety and flexibility defy neat definitions. Yet, pointed questions call for pointed responses. Having already discussed the history and theology of the base church and having looked at its shape within church structures, I now want to move on to interpret base community in terms of its *function*, or behavior.

Let me acknowledge the impossibility of detailing a description which would apply to small groups universally. No two human beings are exactly alike, and neither will any two groups match each other. The composition of the group and its expectations determine its behavior. Variety is the spice of life, even in base groups. This variety provides a richness which I have grown to appreciate.

I recall the first Presbyterian-convened House Church Consultation, which met in Atlanta in 1969. Some practitioners came feeling *their* model was *the* house church! Others, lacking self-assurance, wondered why they had been invited. By the time the consultation ended, however, all had affirmed the basic and central functions of the house church and had recognized the value of diversity of expression.

I find the time-honored three-fold functions of *kerygma* (gospel), *koinonia* (fellowship), and *diaconia* (service) a good handle for analyzing base groups. For our purposes, these three functions will be divided and expanded into nine. We will examine what these are, project their results, and describe "how-to-do-it" options. No one group could undertake all nine functions at each gathering. Healthy groups would, however, incorporate most or all of the functions into their life at one time or another.

1. We pray

For some who are starved for community, the "prayer group" holds little attraction — for them, the name projects visions of routine, impersonal gatherings of pious people, assembled for a limited purpose. In fairness, I must acknowledge that some people who engage in prayer groups are at the same time involved in other church endeavors which round out their spiritual lives. Too, there are many ongoing groups which style themselves "prayer" groups but which actually function more broadly as base community.

It is my impression that prayer groups are waning. I find it interesting that while this decline is taking place, interest in the mystical aspects of life is increasing. For example, thousands of young people (and people not so young) are joining groups for yoga, transcendental meditation, and other disciplines from primitive or eastern religions.

So, prayer is not obsolete! The church must encourage vitality in personal and corporate prayer; also, the church must remember that people have other needs, as well. Fortunately, base-church groups can capture prayer and these other dimensions of Christian life.

The Taizé Community in France maintains creative worship and prayer disciplines three times a day. The ecumenical order at Taizé receives visitors from over the world, including increasing numbers of young people. Sixteen thousand worshiped in Taizé at Easter of 1972. Thousands come weekly. When I asked Brother Leonard why so many come, he replied, "Because we pray." He continued, "Many small cell groups form as a result of attendance here. We see three ingredients which constitute healthy group life. They are: (1) prayer, (2) sharing material possessions, and (3) service outside the group." The Taizé Community's practice of prayer attracts, rather than repels, the world.

I find that people really want to pray but don't know how. Jesus taught his disciples *how* to pray as well as *what* to pray. Most people have limited prayer experiences. They have only listened to public prayers, recited childhood prayers by rote, or expressed yearnings in silent solitude. The mere thought of a participatory, corporate prayer expression terrifies them. But the informal, trusting environment of the base group provides a setting for learning how to pray both individually and corporately. Participants don't have to sit with hands folded and eyes closed, going "in turn" to voice lengthy prayers. Alternative body positions, touching, open-eyed conversations, and one-word "bombardments" are just a few of the optional ways to express our prayers to God.

The standard divisions of prayer have increasing meaning for groups in which I participate. Adoration, confession, thanksgiving, intercession, and petition provide clear categories by which prayer can be built as the group shares out of the past week or anticipates the future. Instead of beginning with a routine opening exercise, one or more of these prayer categories can be used to gather and lift to God the people's experiences and concerns. (This can as easily be done at the conclusion of the meeting.)

How to do it

One-word prayers or phrase prayers. The leader indicates transition from one phase to another — thanksgiving, confession, intercession, etc. Participants focus their expressions into one word or phrase and say it aloud. For prayers of intercession, use only the first names of persons for whom you pray.

Conversational prayer. The group centers on the presence of Christ in their midst, then speaks conversationally, building upon each other's prayers. (See Rosalind Rinker, *Prayer, Conversing with God*.)

Serial prayer. Observe silence, allowing each person to break the silence with an audible prayer. This is a familiar method.

Corporate silence. Observe a lengthy covenant of silence, being aware of the community of faith and one's grounding in the living Christ.

Litany response. For prayers of intercession for others and petition for self, share a concern (eyes open). The group responds to each concern by repeating in unison, "Hear our prayer, O Lord."

Dialogue writing. In a ten-minute covenant of silence, each person writes a dialogue between himself and God over a particular concern, alternating between "me" and "God" quotations. After the writing has been completed, invite members to read or comment on their writing. Allow the right of privacy and nonparticipation.

Nonverbal body prayers. Stand slightly beyond arm's reach of each other with eyes closed. While the leader slowly recites the Lord's Prayer, amplify the prayer through body motion. (Or dance to music.)

Dance prayers. Focus on a concern and a prayer category. Dance the expression with music. (See Marge Champion, *Catch The New Wind.*)

Fantasy role prayer. Stand at arm's length from each other. While background music is playing, close your eyes and imagine that you are a tree in God's world. Feel what trees feel. After about three minutes, tell what you, a tree, would like to say to God.

Body positions. (for silent or spoken prayers.)

(a) Assume a prenatal position for prayers of confession. Or clench your fists. After a declaration of forgiveness, help each other to open up physically and spiritually for assurance of pardon.

(b) Kneel or lie prostrate, with face down to the floor.

(c) Lie on your back, with your head touching the heads of others, thereby forming a wheel. (Your heads are at the hub.) Touch hands and then lift them to form an altar.

(d) Stand in a tight circle facing inward with arms around each other (huddle group). With eyes open, call another person (or each person, in succession) by name, followed by your prayer. "Martha, my prayer for you is . . ." (Make-a-wish style.)

(e) Cradle for intercession. The "subject" lies on his back on the floor. The group gathers around him, then lifts him to waist height and rocks him like a baby. Prayers may be spoken for the person. Conclude by standing him on his feet.

(f) Lay on hands. The members of the group gather around a person and lay their hands on his head, shoulders, or back. Patting or massage may accompany the prayers. The laying on of hands — ordaining and setting apart persons for healing, tasks, ministries, and special functions — is an ancient tradition.

(g) Anoint with oil. Let one person serve as "priest" to the group by applying a drop of scented oil to their foreheads while, at the same time, expressing prayers of intercession.

2. We study

The small group has served long and well as a vehicle for study, but when it is confined to the study-discussion function, it tends to go stale. Head-tripping, brain-storming, and batting ideas back and forth simply reinforce one of the church's problems — namely, we have become too cerebral! Ideas prompt chewing and tasting, but often they are not digested and assimilated.

In the base group, study can be placed in the context of worship, fellowship, and action. These additional elements permit the base community to discover its roots in history and tradition. New communities of faith are not historical accidents. Discovery of the theological, historical, and Biblical tradition provides grounding.

I recall the excitement of visiting the small fishing village in Denmark where my grandfather had lived as a child. My identity was affirmed as I soaked up the environment, visited the church where he was baptized, and fantasized about the courage and bravery of the old Vikings! The base community discovers this same kind of excitement when it walks through history, identifying with a Calvin as he attempted to build a city of faith, justice, and righteousness — or a Paul as he attempted to evangelize Corinth — or a Philemon, who hosted a house church — or a sick man as he begged Jesus to heal him — or the prophet Amos as he cried out against the injustice which the rich inflicted upon the poor. God is the Lord of history, and the church lives in a stream of history. The base group finds its identity as it comes to grips with both its contemporary setting and the Christian tradition. Study and examination of the Biblical and historical record becomes a must.

Study, when pursued within the context of the group's worship and mission, places the process of theologizing within the group. Too often, "doing theology" is relegated to the seminary professor or to a committee charged with the task of writing a new confession of faith. But theologizing can be a very exciting discipline for laymen in small groups. They search for who God is, how he has worked in history, and what a contemporary affirmation of faith looks like.

How to do it

Study the Bible. I recall how a group of my peers were taken aback during a conversation about growth in groups. We were discussing the latest techniques, and a Christian education director observed, "Many of the people I know wouldn't understand what you are talking about. I am amazed, though, to see the growth which takes place when they simply read the Bible together and try to understand what it means!"

Various kinds of aids enrich the study experience. Commentaries and contemporary translations give insight into the historical context and intent of the writer. Well-designed church school materials engage in theological reflection, relating content to personal and social issues. Relational-oriented materials stress group interaction and can be a means of getting into a passage or into the feeling of Biblical characters. (See Lyman Coleman, *Serendipity* Series.[1])

[1]Creative Resources, Word, Inc., 4800 West Waco Drive, Waco, Texas 76703.

Examine books. Economical paperback books place good
material in the hands of the laity. Books should be read outside
the group's meeting time, then discussed. Circulate the reading
material, then give brief reviews of it. Select books on the basis
of the group's expressed goal. For example, a group wrestling
with commitment and an open, honest life style, can read Keith
Miller's *The Taste of New Wine.* A group seeking a specific
ministry can explore what other churches or groups have done.
They might read Elizabeth O'Connor's *Call to Commitment,*
the story of the Church of the Saviour in Washington, D.C.

Explore themes. Select one word or a phrase which focuses
upon a vital topic. This process can be especially effective in
intergenerational groups. Our family hosted an intergenerational
house-church group for nine months. The children helped select
one word for each week. We keyed the music, games, scripture
reading, discussion, role plays, and collage productions to the
theme. Words like "anger," "fear," "love," "friend," and
"peace" provided rich substance for learning experiences which·
were so lively that our children called our sessions "parties."
(For a fuller description of our house church, see Appendix B.)

3. We worship

Groups convene for a variety of reasons. They have different
goals and needs, and differing tasks to perform. The one
distinguishing characteristic of the base church — and of the
church generally — is the practice of worship. Without celebration, the group has no continuity or point of reference outside
itself; over a period of time, it will be reduced to either a sharing
group for "hale fellows well met" or an issue-centered task
force. It will not be a new form of the church.

Worship expresses our response to God. Participants celebrate
his love, grace, and power, along with their own sense of growth
and belonging. Mutual support is engendered in the act of
celebrative worship. "If one member is honored, all rejoice
together." (I Corinthians 12:26 RSV)

In this day of secularism, we have difficulty picturing a
transcendent, personal God; yet he lives in and through the
people in the community of faith. We find God in and through

our fellows, in people who incarnate the spirit of the living God. People can be transformed when the worshiping community expresses warm, trusting, and loving relationships. The small group is a powerful medium in which to worship. Participants can be informed, supported, and forgiven by their neighbors. They can become priests and ministers to each other.

How often do one's real, gut-level feelings get touched in mass worship? If I come to the typical Sunday morning service with a dominant feeling of grief, loneliness, or joy — will I ever get to express it? If I do, how will the other participants react? Many people return home from worship with their feelings left untouched. In a base group, worship addresses the person right where he is. The celebrating community weeps with those who weep and rejoices with those who rejoice. Celebration goes far beyond party-like exuberance. The corporate community addresses and lifts to God the participants' real feelings, whether joy, grief, hurt, or anger.

To design worship which will be meaningful for the base group is a difficult task. "Innovations" soon run stale; the group cannot feed on innovation alone. Shared planning and full participation are much more difficult than passively receiving a regular order which a clergyman-leader "lays on" the congregation. Early in its development, The Church Without Walls in Kansas City struggled with worship patterns. Negative reaction to previous traditional worship experiences had to be faced and worked through. Don Parkinson, the pastor-leader, observed, "We have had to struggle with what worship is, and many people have been involved in leading and designing experiences that can become worship. Few of us are satisfied that we have found the best way to worship, but the struggle in itself is of value and people have moved beyond being spectators in worship."

The possibility for rapid change and variety in worship can be seen in an Episcopal house church in Birmingham, Alabama. The Church of the Transfiguration meets on Sundays for an hour and a half. They have discussions, feed each other communion, and offer spontaneous prayers of thanksgiving and of intercession. Committees experiment with new liturgies. (They have developed twenty-two in the last two years.) Every three months, they lay aside and reevaluate their whole program, including the liturgies; then they negotiate a new three-month covenant.

I cannot overemphasize the possibilities for dynamic worship in base groups; however, I want to keep in perspective and underscore the need for occasional celebrations with masses of people. Many base groups cluster together five to twelve times a year for the "big thing." These celebrations can incorporate some of the spontaneous, participatory flavor of the smaller grouping. The base-group style of worship finds expression in the larger mix.

How to do it

People engaged in new worship forms need to know why they are doing what they are doing. They should be able to relate the new to the old, the innovative to the traditional, in a conceptual framework. Examination of the old orders of worship and contemporary orders will reveal certain elements in common. Let's look at a traditional order, then consider variations.

(1) The call to worship

In a traditional order, the pastor announces the call (or invitation) to worship from the pulpit. In the base group, the members greet each other, extending words of welcome. "This is the day the Lord has made, let's rejoice and be happy in it." Or, "The Lord is risen . . . He is risen indeed!" Paul gives us a clue to the lively welcome to worship which the first house-church Christians extended: He encouraged them to greet each other with a holy kiss. Come to think of it, an embrace is really a very direct call to worship. For one thing, the leader does not get all the attention; it is passed around within the community!

(2) Invocation

Prayers of invocation affirm who God is and who we are. Direct, participatory, one-word prayers can summarize the affirmations and feelings of the group. Additional methods, such as silence, fantasy trips, and single-word expressions, quickly bring concerns to the surface.

Prayers can be sung. Use the African spiritual "Kum Ba Yah"

(meaning "come by here"), pausing between each verse to allow someone to articulate in one word how he feels. The group can respond: "Elmer feels troubled, (Suzie feels thankful . . . Joyce feels hopeful). Oh, Lord, come by here." This acknowledges who we are and brings who we are to God.

An extended "logging in" (accounting of what has happened since the last meeting), followed by a summary prayer, gives worship a lively start. Stress the importance of *new* information, not a rehash of the old. The New Testament practice of prophecy refers to reporting what God is and has been doing, as well as foretelling what he will do in the future.

(3) Prayers

Thanksgiving, confession, intercession, and petition have been discussed under the function of prayer. Shared participation which touches the "closet" concerns — the needs and dreams of people — has vitality. Provide a relaxed or flexible framework into which people can insert their own agenda of interests and concerns.

As a pastor, I found the pastoral prayer the most frustrating aspect of worship for which to prepare. I simply couldn't know what was deep inside several hundred people unless there happened to be a national, community, or family event which obviously dominated their minds. Prayers which I prepared on Saturday could be made obsolete by unpredictable events of the next twenty-four hours.

(4) Praise

In addition to the use of a familiar hymnbook, there's the option of a three-ring notebook into which new hymns may be inserted. The book then becomes an account of the history of the group. Many folk hymns with easy, singable tunes are available. They can be sung without accompaniment or with guitar. Some groups buy records and sing along.

With a little practice, the group can learn "portable" responses which relate various worship activities. Multiple-use music includes the various forms of "Amen," such as the three-fold amen or the "Amen" from *The Lilies of the Field*; the Kyrie eleison ("Lord have mercy upon us, Christ have mercy upon us"), and trinitarian praises (the "Gloria Patri" or "Doxology") set to familiar tunes.

Joining as a group to write hymns is an exciting adventure
for base churches. Many Psalms lend themselves to the construction of new tunes or to coupling with established tunes.

(5)   Affirmation of faith

Traditionally, we recite the Apostles' Creed or, perhaps, the
Nicene Creed. Other historic creeds forged out of the struggle
of God's people can be included in a loose-leaf binder. In
addition, the group can articulate its own beliefs. Invite each
person, in turn, to state in one sentence what he believes. (What
do *you* believe?) Selected scripture can also be used to affirm
one's faith.

(6)   The Word

The Bible provides an unparalleled record of how God acts
and who he is, as revealed in Jesus Christ. The first-century
house church gathered to read the Old Testament and the
circulating letters of the apostles. The Reformation made the
Word central to worship. The Word was to be read and explained
in language understood by the people.

Proclamation of the Word in base groups may take place as a
leader teaches the Bible, as the group engages in dialogue, or as
the group listens to tapes recorded by preachers or teachers.

(7)   The Sacraments

During a retreat, the elements of communion were passed
from person to person, along with the instructions, "Share with
each other the bread and in your own words the 'good news.' "
When Gloria received the bread, she broke into tears. "For
thirty-five years," she said, "I have participated in communion,
but it has always been another person's (the preacher's) good
news." The force and power of the simple act of ministering to
each other opened up the gospel in a new way to her.

Most denominations require the presence of an ordained
clergyman for an authorized service of communion or baptism.
The existence of multiple new forms of the church calls for a
new look at ordination and sacramental rules. For instance, if
an authentic conversion takes place in a base group, why
wouldn't baptism be located there? The base group would
become the community of "God parents."

The practice of communion in the house church can have tremendous impact, but why must a clergyman be present? Couldn't church councils authorize laymen to preside at the small-group communion? I believe that a change in denominational regulations is in order. (The United Presbyterian Church is, in fact, considering such a change.) If small groups can meet without a pastor for the purpose of Bible study, prayer, and mission planning, why not for the eucharist? The change from the early church's common-meal communion to large congregational communion has altered not only the practice, but also the *meaning* of the sacrament. Individualism and clergy-centeredness within congregations have replaced the intimacy and corporateness of the household. John Tanburn traces the practice of the early church:

> In the earliest days we know of *no settled rule*, even concerning the *Breaking of Bread*. If there was a convention in some local churches that only an elder might preside at the eucharist, it was not sufficiently important even to gain a mention in the otherwise detailed sacramental regulations sent by Paul to the chaotic church at Corinth. Clement, Bishop of Rome towards the end of the first century, wrote a long letter to the Corinthians in which he likened the apostles, presbyter/bishops and deacons to the High Priest, priests and Levites of the Old Covenant, and required members of the church to keep to their proper functions. Yet presidency at the eucharist is not mentioned. The Didache also has detailed sacramental regulations — without limiting who may offer the thanksgiving. We have to wait for the second century, after all the apostles have died, to find any limitations at all; and even then it is not restricted entirely to the local ordained minister or bishop; Ignatius, bishop of Antioch, wrote to the Christians at Smyrna, 'Let that be considered a valid eucharist over which the bishop presides, *or one to whom he commit it*'. The presbyter/bishops have not yet taken over all the ministrations of the Spirit, and some of them ruled without teaching or preaching as late as Cyprian. So far from depressing the lay body into a passive dependence on them, the ministers saw their function as 'to equip God's people for work in his services' (Ephesians 4:12, NEB) — to stimulate and train them in corporate fellowship and mission.[2]

2John Tanburn, *Open House* (London: Falcon Books, 1970), p. 32.

So, what guidelines should be followed? Without authoriza-
tion a group may conduct love feasts or agape meals in which
bread may be broken and shared. Regarding communion, if you
choose to follow denominational policies (where these apply),
secure permission or the presence of an ordained clergyman to
officiate. Finally, work to remove restrictions which bar laymen
from serving and sharing communion in authorized groups.

  (8) Offering

Offerings include far more than what is placed in a money
plate passed by boutonniered ushers. Any base group can find
convenient ways to collect money, but finding a ritual whereby
we can offer ourselves to God and his work is more difficult.
Can we find ways to declare our intentions to the community?
What am I willing to be and do with or for you? Psychologists
are increasingly placing stress on the role of intentional living.
The offering provides a good opportunity for intentions to be
declared. Both support and accountability are practiced in the
community of faith.

Place a sheet of newsprint on the floor in the center of the
group. Let individuals, couples, families, or the corporate group
write what they offer in view of everyone.

A covenant of silence can provide a setting in which each
person writes a dialogue with God on "the offering or covenant
which I make." Invite members to read about their covenant as
an act of offering (but do not insist).

Writing a corporate covenant can help the group to focus on
clear goals and purposes. The Agora community in Minneapolis
writes both individual and corporate covenants every three
months. They cover the four areas of nurture, worship, fellowship, and service. Incorporating the offering into the worship
service as a liturgical act is most appropriate.

Standard covenants can be borrowed. My favorite is found
in the *Book of Common Worship* of the Church of South India.

> I am no longer my own, but thine. Put me to what thou wilt,
> rank me with whom thou wilt; put me to doing, put me to
> suffering; let me be employed for thee or laid aside for thee,
> exalted for thee or brought low for thee; let me be full, let me
> be empty; let me have all things, let me have nothing; I freely
> and heartily yield all things to thy pleasure and disposal.

54656

And now, O glorious and blessed God, Father, Son, and Holy
Spirit, thou art mine, and I am thine. So be it. And the
covenant which I have made on earth, let it be ratified in
Heaven.[3]

(9) Benediction

The benediction provides a way for the group to say good-by
and to wish one another God's peace.

The ancient tradition of "passing the peace" suits base communities to a "T." The members clasp each other's hands, and
each one, in turn, says, "May the peace of God be with you."

The group can huddle, with hands clasped or with arm linked
in arm. With eyes open, they repeat together any one of several
familiar benedictions, which they have memorized. One is:

> May the Lord bless you and keep you,
> May the Lord make his face to shine
> upon you and be gracious unto you;
> May the Lord lift up the light of
> His countenance upon you
> And give you peace! Amen.

The song "Shalom, My Friends" can be sung while the participants shake hands, nod heads, or hug a farewell. "Shalom"
(meaning *peace*, or *well-being*) may be spoken as a benediction.
Some groups borrow the "Om" practice from yoga groups.
While sitting in a circle with clasped hands, or packed together
in a standing "love ball," the participants can sing "Shalom" or
hum to a loud crescendo, letting it die away slowly. People feel
the benediction as it is pronounced in humming vibrations
emitted by the family of God.

4. We tend

Jesus instructed his disciples to "tend my sheep." What did
he mean? The dictionary meaning of "tend" suggests the act of
caring for or watching over. In the base group, the tending
activity takes the shape of accepting, listening to, and affirming

[3]The Church of South India, *The Book of Common Worship* (London:
Oxford University Press, 1963), p. 137.

the other person. He is valued and ministered to as a unique human being.

A layman in Kansas City who had started twenty-two small groups was asked the secret of his success. He replied, "We have learned the discipline of consciously celebrating the uniqueness of each other."

The base church which feels the suffering of one person has met the first standard of a healing community. Persons are liberated and loved into wholeness. Beyond that, they gain a sense of power and usefulness, for their gifts are called forth by the community. How many laymen have good intentions for ministry, but feel inadequate! When they move into small groups, they begin to come alive and they discover gifts of which they were unaware. These gifts include wisdom and understanding; powers of healing; practical and prophetic insights; abilities to listen, talk, and teach; capabilities to lead, amuse, and administer — and who knows what else? The Biblical enumeration of God's gifts to the "body" through the Holy Spirit are only suggestive, certainly not exhasutive!

In a society where the sounds of impersonal silence prevail for many, effective listening has tremendous power. Tending through listening is more feasible in small groups than in larger gatherings.

Frequently, we imagine the strong Christian as the one who *performs* ministry. Many who follow this line (especially pastors) become overburdened because they seldom express their own needs and *receive* ministry from others. Ministering is a two-way street. A seminary professor recommends this test for determining whether or not a student is ready for ministry: "Can the student permit others to minister to him?"

I personally experience the best two-way ministering within a house church. There I move beyond the leader role and share my need, allowing the group to minister to me. How often do we avail ourselves of the opportunity to help others by permitting them to help us?

How to do it

Have the group discuss a given question and instruct all

participants to listen closely to one another. Then assign partners. Ask each partner to repeat what the other person said in the larger group. (Be careful to capture the feelings behind the words as well.) How important we feel when we are quoted — we have really counted with someone. We have been heard! The expectancy I observe in people as they hear their "playback" reveals the power of this simple exercise.

Provide each person with a 3 x 5 card. Give a pencil to one member and ask him to record his own gifts and strengths as the group voices them. Then pass the pencil to another person and have the group identify his gifts. This "bombardment" exercise may confirm gifts which persons lacked the boldness to appropriate or express.

A role play is another method. It provides an opportunity to live in someone else's shoes. For many persons, the ability to empathize comes very slowly.

5. We disclose

The only way I can ever be known by another person is to reveal myself to him. I have to "grow my person" inside him. If I hide myself, retreat behind my masks, and play games, I will not experience the world. Authentic persons face themselves honestly and thereby come to a realistic knowledge of themselves. The thesis of Sidney Jourard's book *The Transparent Self* is, "No man can come to know himself unless he discloses himself to another person." The small group should not deteriorate into a confessional of past "sins." Self-understanding can come through sharing present attitudes and feelings. One will share only as deeply as the level of trust which has been established. Jourard elaborates:

> A person will disclose himself only when he believes that his audience is a man of good will. To put this another way, self-disclosure follows an attitude of love and trust. If I love someone, not only do I strive to know him, so that I can devote myself more effectively to his well-being; I also display my love by letting him know me. At the same time by so doing, I permit him to love me.[4]

[4]Sidney M. Jourard, *The Transparent Self* (Princeton, N. J.: D. Van Nostrand Co., 1964), p. 4.

Sharing who I am gives me a chance to formulate my own story and to have the uniqueness of my history affirmed by the group. My story includes emotions of fear, anger, and pain which I have internalized. In his "Shalom" retreats, Jerry Jud has developed a methodology which focuses on getting "blocking" emotions out and into the community of people, who have covenanted to love each other. Afterward, participants attest to a new sense of liberation and joy, and an ability to express love.

An example of the effect of story-telling in a loving group is related by R. J. Lavin, pastor of St. Paul's Lutheran Church in Davenport, Iowa:

> I have frequently referred to one of the Koinonia groups without telling the leaders what the problems are, but that the new members need some support as persons . . . In one case I referred a rape victim, let's call her Mary, to a small group after I had met with her over a period of about two months with little progress in her gaining self-esteem. No matter what I said to Mary, she seemed unable to regain her feeling of dignity as a woman and as a Christian until I asked her to join a small group. I don't know how much of her story she told the group, but I do know this — she is a changed woman, completely different than the cowering woman who first told me that she was not clean. She needed and got support, love, and acceptance, which I think she never could have gotten from a counsellor, at least not to the same extent she had her needs met by a Koinonia group.[5]

Self-disclosure can also point to the future. Sam Keen describes the sharing of one's history as *grounding* and the sharing of one's dreams as *soaring*. He suggests that the church has failed on both accounts. *What is your dream, your vision? What youthful dreams have you shelved?* The creative process begins with dreaming and imagining, then moves to decision and action. Both children and the insane have much to teach us. They dare to dream!

The Old Testament prophet observed, "Where there is no vision, the people perish." The word of the Lord at Pentecost

---

[5]R. J. Lavin, *Koinonia Groups: A Strategy for Penetration* (unpublished pamphlet), p. 12.

was, "Your young men will see visions and your old men will dream dreams." The creative process begins when persons dare to tell their inner, hidden hopes without fear of rejection or ridicule.

Honesty breeds trust and more honesty. Nowhere is this more apparent than in intergenerational groups. Art Foster, of Chicago Theological Seminary, observes this:

> Also fascinating is the manner in which total family units have been included in the housechurch process, especially at times of high holidays. This accords with one of our own findings and with that of family therapists, that children and young people can function very well in the atmosphere of openness and honest communication with adults. Far from needing protection from the truth of older persons, such as their parents, they already know far more than adults think. They can deal with meanings much more creatively when their parents are open and honest in their presence.[6]

How to do it

No function opens the door to misuse and abuse more than does self-disclosure. Groups bog down in the mire of introspection if their only function is self-disclosure and therapy based on past history. Moreover, various tricks and gimmicks aimed at "opening people up" become manipulative and invade rights to privacy. People get seduced into self-disclosure by the patterns of others who "share." The desire to be included pushes them into playing the game even if they are not ready for it.

Some suggestions:

(1) As a rule, let the trust level of the group regulate the amount of disclosure. The National Training Labs have discovered that even the best and most reputable group leaders have casualties. Participants trust the leader (especially an author) as an authority more than they trust their relationship with him as a person. They "dump" more information and feelings than their inner regulators ordinarily permit them to share; consequently, they go beyond any leader's ability to

[6]Arthur L. Foster, "The House Church: Context and Form," *The Chicago Theological Seminary Register* (December, 1970), pp. 27-28.

preserve their emotional stability. Usually, people have a "sense" of how much to share. Let that sense govern. A style of complete honesty and openness cannot become the rule for every group meeting.

Cross-examination (the use of "why" words) should be avoided. People should be given the freedom to say "Stop" or "I pass." The group should honor this inclination.

(2) Leading questions can be used if they leave multiple options for responding; they should not demand a specific response. Do not ask people to describe a "most (whatever it is) experience." Some opening questions which I have found useful are:

> Describe your house (draw a floor plan), showing the center of warmth.
>
> Describe a person who was influential in your life and what made him so?
>
> In what (or in whom) did you find childhood security?
>
> Share an experience of joy, or wholeness.   '
>
> Share an experience of "community."
>
> Share an experience or observation of God working in human life.
>
> Relate how your ambitions or attitudes have changed within the last two years.
>
> Describe a turning point in your life. Relate any dynamics of the Christian faith which may have been involved.
>
> Share an experience of ministry on either the giving or the receiving end.
>
> What turns you on?
>
> Share a surprise!

(3) Fantasy may be used to help people get in touch with their inner thoughts. Perceptions should be quickly stated for focus purposes but not dwelt upon or analyzed.

(4) "Differential perception" triggers feedback. Ask each member to state simply: (a) how I see myself, (b) how I see you, and (c) how I think you see me. When each person has written these impressions, they can be shared.

6. We share

In America, growth groups, prayer groups, and sharing groups deal with almost every aspect of life except *money*. In Europe, many "new-form" Christian communities contract to share some quantity of money with each other. Their patterns may have implications for American base churches. Brother Leonard of Taizé insists that a necessary requirement of Christian cells is the sharing of material possessions. He would not impose strict demands — each group has to work out a covenant for themselves. New experiments in shared living abound. When participants live under one roof and share all of their earnings, the Europeans call them "full living" groups. If they do not live in the same building but have negotiated a sharing agreement, they are called "half living" groups!

In America, groups are experimenting with sharing material possessions. The Episcopal Church of the Redeemer in Houston, Texas, has twenty-seven extended-family "households" which form the backbone of the congregation. The Hollywood (California) United Presbyterian Church initiated new sharing communities for young adults. A group of nondenominational house-church practitioners wrestled in a retreat at Kirkridge over the question, "What social living arrangements need to be constructed for our day?"

Frequently, the base of support for Jesus People is a communal experience. All of these experiences say loud and clear that trust, faith, care, support, and sharing soon get down to the nitty-gritty of things and money.

People in base communities, too, develop a keen sense of stewardship. Since most base groups are not locked into building construction and maintenance costs, resources are freed for mission. While per capita giving of the Presbyterian denominations runs a bit more than $100 per capita, giving in the Presbyterian-related Church Without Walls in Kansas City was $353!

How to do it

(1) Assess dues for each "unit" (single adult, couple, or

family), perhaps on a monthly basis. Some groups charge from $10 to $25 per month.

(2)   Give through volunteer offerings and pledges.

(3)   Have each person covenant to share a stated percentage of his income. The members of a house group near Neushatel, Switzerland, share 20 percent of their incomes. Some of the money is used for group needs, but most is given away for specific ministries.

(4)   A maximum need for each family unit can be set, based on the national average income. The remainder of the participants' income goes to the community. The Shadwell group in England experimented along these lines.

(5)   Income and property can be maintained separately, but be shared freely on the basis of need. A Catholic group in Brussels operates this way. A student in the community is being put through college by the base group.

(6)   Sharing in the preparation of corporate meals provides an opportunity to invite outsiders for sharing and conversations. Some groups in Europe meet weekly for their own study, worship, and planning, then meet an additional time around a common meal with invited guests. They see this occasion as an opportunity to witness.

(7)   Communal (full living) arrangements require much maintenance and thus entail effort and time, but they provide a constant context of community into which a person with needs can be brought — he doesn't have to wait until Thursday evening or Sunday morning for someone to pray with him or to share food and counsel with him.

Communal arrangements should provide adequate private family space. One base group is exploring the possibility of buying some acreage, building a central activities-meeting house, and placing mobile homes for the participating families around this central building.

The Kauchema community in Kansas City purchased an apartment house. They rent out the first floor and use the remainder of the building for family living and community gatherings. One apartment is reserved for use by a person needing a continuing live-in ministry.

The future living patterns for new types of base communities are not yet clear. Much experimentation remains to be done. We can predict that the future will hold variety.

7. We explore

As we move to consider the *diaconia* (service) dimension of the group, we identify and understand the needs and hurts of the world. Many groups have developed a contract of personal growth and mutual support but have difficulty turning the corner into ministry and outreach. Can the group exist for the benefit of persons on its outside? Ministry to the world is part and parcel of the church's life. If the base group wants to be called "church," it must bear the mark of ministry.

Needs and opportunities in the world shape the strategies and actions. So much hurt exists! The victims include both the *down*-and-outer and the *up*-and-outer. The group must survey, reduce, and select. The magnitude and weight of the problems can so overwhelm the group that they will never get started. But start they must, for in addition to its inherent good, mission is also the only preventive for introversion.

How to do it

Needs that we only read about hold their distance; those with which we have personal contact evoke emotional responses. Devise schemes to establish personal relationships through which the issues that affect people's lives can be discovered.

(1) Invite others to visit your group — either persons with special needs or those who are conversant about the specific needs of others.

(2) Volunteer for special community service and report back what you discover. (Establishing a relationship with a welfare recipient and transporting his food-stamp groceries give a new and informative view of the welfare trap.)

(3) In your home, host people who are different from you. The L'Abri fellowship in Switzerland has developed a significant ministry to young people; it is a teaching ministry, but also a ministry of hosting strangers from over the world. In his book *The Church at the End of the 20th Century* Francis Schaeffer gives few clues for the emerging church's "shape" other than to

insist that it have New Testament marks. He does, however, propose a starting place for evangelical Christians — an open home.

> In about the first three years of L'Abri all our wedding presents were wiped out. Our sheets were torn. Holes were burned in our rugs. Indeed once a whole curtain almost burned up from somebody smoking in our living room. Blacks came to our table. Orientals came to our table. Everybody came to our table. It couldn't happen any other way. Drugs came to our place. People vomited in our rooms, in the rooms of Chalet Les Melezes which was our home, and now in the rest of the Chalets of L'Abri.
>
> How many times has this happened to you? You see, you don't need a big program. You don't have to convince your session or board. All you have to do is open your home and begin. And there is no place in God's world where there are no people who will come and share a home as long as it is a real home.
>
> How many times have you risked an unantiseptic situation by having a girl who might easily have a sexual disease sleep between your sheets? We have girls come to our homes who have three or four abortions by the time they are 17. Is it possible they have veneral disease? Of course. But they sleep between our sheets. How many times have you let this happen in your home? Don't you see this is where we must begin? This is what the love of God means. This is the admonition to the elder — that he must be given to hospitality. Are you an elder? Are you given to hospitality? If not, keep quiet. There is no use talking. But you can begin.[7]

(4) Play simulation games. One woman who had no sympathy whatsoever for prostitutes had second thoughts following a simulation game in which circumstances forced her into the role of a prostitute — she had to be one to survive. Her emotions became wrapped up in a role outside of herself.

(5) Engage in role plays.

(6) See a movie together and then discuss it.

(7) Listen to pop-rock music. Music is the communications

[7]Francis Schaeffer, *The Church at the End of the 20th Century* (Downers Grove, Ill.: Inter-Varsity Press, 1970), p. 108.

medium for young people. Ask the teenagers in your group to teach you through records what youth are thinking and feeling.

8. We strategize

The planning process cannot be viewed as a new messiah for the church because without motivation and support, it is little more than a routine exercise. But adequate plans, objectives, and evaluation are important to the base group; they provide direction and movement.

Decision-making by the whole group helps to frame the covenant which is foundational to group life. If the base group functions in relation to a cluster or to another church body, a total strategy can be developed out of the parts.

How to do it

Strategizing incorporates these components:

(1) *State the goal.* If the goal aims to solve a problem, state the problem — then restate the goal by describing the change which must take place.

(2) *Explore alternative steps* that could be taken to reach the goal.

(3) *Weigh the consequences* of each option and the resources (time, know-how, money) available to pursue each option.

(4) *Decide on one option.* Organize around that decision. Let each member state an intention relative to the task. The intention can be adjusted as a part of the covenanting process.

(5) *Act on the decision.* The group may act corporately or individually, or two or three members can yoke for a specific task.

(6) *Report and evaluate* "how it went." Deal with the real feelings of those who report. Revise plans on the basis of each evaluation. The contents of the evaluation can become grist for the worship experience.

9. We act

The planning process propels the base group into action beyond itself. By listing action last, I am not necessarily recommending a sequence of order. Some groups follow the study-fellowship-action sequence, but the order can be varied. The total style of the group is what counts. If the group waits until all of its members have been changed, healed, and supported before it begins to reach out to others, it will never move. Many people find healing by giving themselves to others.

The old tension between individual and corporate expressions of ministry raises its head when the group thinks about action. Some churches insist that each base group have a corporate mission project and that each member pull his share of the load. When this rule applies, some very busy people who are already located in crucial decision points of society may drop out; they feel they already have a ministry where they are, and they want the group to recognize it, legitimate it, and support them in it. Why not design the missional function of the base community to embrace both dimensions? A corporate ministry can be adopted with an understanding that individuals will involve themselves in varying degrees. Each person would, however, declare his ministry covenant for the review of the community. Their counsel and support would be built into the weekly "log-in," discussion, and worship.

How to do it

No one mission avenue can be imposed upon the group; therefore, let's look at several examples.

Trinity Presbyterian Church in Harrisonburg, Virginia, builds its life around house churches. Each house church operates a specific ministry — a coffee house, clothes closet, drama ministry, ministry to prisons, and ministry to retarded children. Each house church accounts to the session of the church through their elder representative, and annually each church terminates its life. New house churches are called into being each September.

The Three Chopt Presbyterian Church in Richmond, Virginia, projects annually a list of varying house-church opportunities, from study to growth to action. The dialogue house church, for instance, attempts to reach across racial and economic lines in a ministry of reconciliation.

The First Presbyterian Church of Berkeley, California, lists fourteen different task forces in which people can express ministry. They include Free Church, Big Brothers, jobs, literacy, tutoring, pre-school, books, friendship visitation, international hospitality, prayer, music, and nurture.

A Christian commune in Jacksonville, Florida, led by Jim Hornsby, designates work and ministry tasks for each member. The members helped Jim win a spot on the school board. They work with an Afro-American industries project which is designed to help poor people. Some of the members do street evangelism, including working with young people who are on drugs.

Community Of Active Christians Today (COACT), organized in 1970 in Waco, Texas, is characterized by shared leadership, weekly celebrations in homes, and personal growth in groups. Members are involved in community affairs and world affairs. Thirty different programs outside the COACT system have received their support, either collectively or individually. They aim to use one-half of their money for COACT maintenance and the other half for people-oriented programs in the Waco community.

The Sycamore Community in State College, Pennsylvania, consciously attempts to develop the inward and outward journey. Their descriptive brochure indicates they are "up to" programs in everyday mental health; science, technology and the church; and sex ethics. Without the strain of maintaining a building and paying other overhead, their giving is channeled to ministries in the urban ghetto; to alleviating world poverty; to retreat and education centers, and to the National Council of Churches and the World Council of Churches.

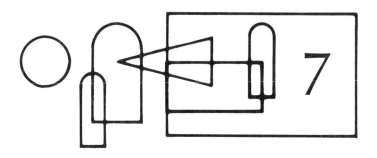

LEADERSHIP MODELS
FOR BASE GROUPS

Proposals for the formation and legitimation of base communities within church structures are not enough to make renewal happen. Like the drunk who saw the Washington Monument for the first time and observed, "You'll never get that rocket off the ground," so the base group needs life and fire!

Form should follow life, not the other way around. Usually, when you find a group that is really alive, you also find a committed and sensitive leader or a core of similarly endowed leaders.

In 1972, while doing a survey of new forms of Christian community in Europe, I noted that behind every effective group was a leader — a dreamer who could communicate with people and who was both trusted and trusting. So, if we think strategically about an effective, high-quality base for the church, the first step is to locate good leadership material, then equip them for the task.

We sometimes hear, "If we could only form into small groups where everyone is a leader, we would no longer need professional leadership, and the church could function much more efficiently." I don't believe it! If the present church were restructured into an organism of cellular base groups, it would need *more* leadership, not less. To rely on a shared leadership, and perhaps a leadership reduced to the lowest common denominator of awareness and competency, would soon leave the church with a multitude of dead cells! In the future, we will need more leadership and a different style of leadership.

In the past, the Quaker movement relied on shared leadership, allowing people to be moved by the Spirit. They continue to affirm this principle, but now they also provide training for church professionals. While the Quakers recognize the need for competent professional leadership, the Lay Renewal Movement in mainline denominations has focused attention on the place and role of shared lay leadership. Interestingly, the writings of Elton Trueblood, a Quaker, have become a rallying cry for a remarkable number of non-Quakers in the Lay Renewal Movement.

Over the years, the pattern of church leadership has generally been authoritarian. The centralization of power began in the third and fourth centuries, when the church started gathering in large assemblies rather than in households. The bishops began governing large congregations on a regional basis instead of coordinating networks of small cells as they formerly did. Limiting the celebration of the mass to a priest and developing the clergy as a closed group with special, ordained functions reinforced the one-way, from-the-top-down leadership patterns.

In the Dark Ages, before the arrival of the printing press, only the clergy read the Bible. Following the Reformation, the clergyman generally continued to be the best educated person in town. He was a man of letters, knowledgeable in science, economics, and history. He was a trusted authority. Church architecture and worship still reflect the authoritarian stance.

With the rise of denominationalism, many competent clergymen rose to the "top." Headquarters cranked out myriad schemes and programs to be passed down through the church for implementation.

All this has left the church with what Jerry Jud calls the "Big Daddy fantasy and the trickle down theory."[1] The church wants "Big Daddy" (the clergyman) to fix everything, and he is

[1] Jerry Jud, "The 'Big Daddy' Fantasy," *Crisis in the Church: Essays in Honor of Truman B. Douglass* (Philadelphia: Pilgrim Press, 1968).

often seduced into thinking he can. He sets goals, plans implementation, and attempts to motivate everyone to follow. Those
who don't buy his program sit on the sidelines and wait for the
next pastor to come along.

Let's be realistic: The Big Daddy days are gone. Parishioners
are no longer semiliterate. The church and the world call for
leaders who stand alongside the people, not above. The new
leader struggles to help the people discover for themselves where
God leads rather than issuing pronouncements from a removed
position. He asks, "Who are you? What do you want to become?
What are your gifts?" He enables persons to discover their
identity and God's call; then he helps them to express their call
in ministry.

The skills required for an enabling (as opposed to authoritarian) leadership demand training that few clergymen have
acquired. In my own early pastoral practice, I leaned toward
being a priestly "Big Daddy" because that was the function for
which I had been educated. The base church of the future will
still require professionals, but with expanded competency in
the dynamics of growth and change in individuals, in church
systems, and in society. New insights from the behavioral
sciences are opening the doors for expanded leadership capabilities.

The most effective leadership posture is not a simple choice
between an authoritarian style, on the one hand, and an enabling
style, on the other. The authoritarian says, "I'll tell you what
to do," while the extremist enabler says, "Do what you want!"
The leadership style must be geared to where the group is.
Groups with high dependency needs will become insecure with
the enabler, while highly autonomous groups will rebel against
the authoritarian. If a leader can develop versatility (taking into
consideration his own behavior, limitations, and strengths), he
can function out of a style appropriate to the given setting. He
can help groups to move gradually from dependency toward
mature autonomy.

The following scale illustrates the interrelation of the group's
behavior and the leader's style.

LEADER/GROUP RELATIONSHIP

Leader Authoritarian	Tells	Sells	Offers	Consults	Participates	Enabling
Group Dependent						Autonomous
	Accepts	Buys	Considers	Plans	Initiates	

A friend who pastored a heady, action-oriented experimental base group struggled with the members for over a year as they planned their own life, worship, and mission. His evaluation read, "The leadership style which I chose was weighed far too much toward the enabling role and not directive enough." Most pastors, however, sin on the other end of the scale!

Although most of my references have been directed to pastors, the buck does not stop there. Many lay leaders are "little pastors." Their church-school teaching methods, for example, reflect the authoritarian approach — the class lines up in rows before the teacher's lecture stand. Our whole system is shot through with the "trickle down" approach — a one-way flow of information and planning.

So, what qualities are we looking for in both the lay and professional leadership of the base-style church? The issue goes deeper than merely acquiring new techniques. The whole person and his attitudes come into play. If the leader creates a climate of trust, he lays a foundation for growth and development, but if he creates an unfriendly climate, the group members will fear ridicule or embarrassment.

The leader must have a good attitude about himself. The good leader knows his gifts. He has a feeling of power, yet recognizes his limitations. He feels "OK" about who he is! He is secure enough to tolerate differences and ambiguity. He knows his values and motivation. In short, he can be himself.

Psychologists and counselors have learned the importance of the personhood of the leader. He cannot be a cool, detached technician, but must instead be willing to engage his total person with another person. Sidney Jourard points out:

> Recent studies, summarized by Carl Rogers (1958), have shown that it is not the technique or the theoretical orientation of the therapist which fosters growth of the sort I have been describing. Rather it is the manner of the therapist's being when in the presence of the patient. *Effective* therapists seem to follow this implicit hypothesis: If they are themselves in the presence of the patient, avoiding *compulsions* to silence, to reflection, to interpretation, to impersonal technique, and kindred character disorders, but instead striving to know their patient, involving themselves in his situation, and then responding to his utterances with their spontaneous selves, this fosters growth. In short, they love their patients. They employ their powers in the service of their patient's well-being and growth, not inflict them on him. Somehow there is a difference.
>
> But this loving relationship is a far cry from the impersonal administration of reflections, interpretations, or the equivalent of pellets. The loving therapist is quite free and spontaneous in his relationship; his responses are bound only by his ethics and his judgment. He may laugh, scold, become angry, give advice — in short, break most of the rules laid down in psychotherapy training manuals . . . It is my growing opinion, somewhat buttressed by accumulating experience in my own therapeutic work, that valued change — growth — in patients is fostered when the therapist is a rather free individual functioning as a person with all of his feelings and fantasies as well as his wits.[2]

In the second place, the leader must have good attitudes about others. He must be able to see and honor the uniqueness of each person. The leader must feel that each person has something to offer to the group, and he must help that person to be heard without fear of rejection. He must also help to weave the person's identity and gifts into the fabric of the community.

[2]Sidney Jourard, *The Transparent Self* (Princeton, N. J.: D. VanNostrand Co., 1964), pp. 62-63.

The group can then be released to develop responsible behavior. Jesus possessed this capacity for liberating people.

Douglas McGregor sees leadership attitudes from the perspective of management. In *The Human Side of Enterprise,* he identifies two distinct management views which relate to two divergent assumptions about human behavior.[3]

Theory X says:

1. The average human being has an inherent dislike of work and will avoid it if he can.
2. Because of the human characteristic of dislike of work, most people must be coerced, controlled, directed, threatened with punishment to get them to put forth adequate effort toward the achievement of organizational objectives.
3. The average human being prefers to be directed, wishes to avoid responsibility, has relatively little ambition, wants security above all.

Theory X calls for an authoritarian role in which the employee is dependent upon the manager.

Theory Y states:

1. The expenditure of physical and mental effort in work is as natural as play or rest.
2. External control and the threat of punishment are not the only means for bringing about effort toward organizational objectives. Man will exercise self-direction and self-control in the service of objectives to which he is committed.
3. Commitment to objectives is related to the rewards associated with their achievement.
4. The average human being learns, under proper conditions, not only to accept but to seek responsibility.
5. The capacity to exercise a relatively high degree of imagination, ingenuity, and creativity in the solution of organizational objectives is widely, not narrowly, distributed in the population.
6. Under the conditions of modern industrial life, the intellectual potentialities of the average human being are only partially utilized.

[3]Douglas McGregor, *The Human Side of Enterprise* (New York: McGraw-Hill, 1961).

This theory is based on generalizations drawn from the insights of the social sciences. Theory Y is more dynamic than theory X, more optimistic about the possibility for human growth and development, more concerned with self-direction and self-responsibility. It pushes the leader in the direction of an enabling role.

The qualities which make for loving, trusting leadership have deep roots in the Christian tradition. Biblical teachings and accounts of Jesus' helping his followers to develop qualities of humanness and godliness provide modern Christians with a unique heritage and direction.

Finding Them, Training Them, and Deploying Them
1. Pastors

The pastor is the key to forging a creative church of base communities. If he holds the congregation to the status quo — if he perches atop the pyramid and sits there feeding his ego — he can block creative movement. But if he can discover new skills and ways of leading, he can open countless doors for people. When people ask for the bread of community, he can either choose to give them the stone of impersonal congregational collectivism or help them to taste the bread of loving community. Many leaders lack skills for building strong, healthy community, so (quite understandably) they do what they know best — they provide command-type leadership.

The obvious place to train for new leadership styles is in the seminaries, and this is beginning to happen, although many seminaries still give more emphasis to history and theology than to mission skills. An experience/reflection context utilizing small working groups is beginning to work its way into the seminaries.

For those thousands of clergymen who are beyond the seminaries, a massive retraining program is in order. The training must run deeper than the usual continuing education update. (Mr. Clergy listens to lectures and assembles new information to pass down to his parishioners when he gets back home.) Pastoral retraining should include an evaluation of skills, behavior, and leadership style, along with a short-range and long-range training prescription. Future training will be located both on and off campus.

Good retraining programs for clergy exist outside the seminaries. Examples are:

The National Council of Churches Training Labs, held at Green Lake, Wisconsin.

The Advanced Pastoral Training Institute, Bloomfield Hills, Michigan, Reuel Howe, director.

Interpreter's House, Lake Junaluska, North Carolina, Carlyle Marney, director.

The Yokefellow Institute, Richmond, Indiana, Sam Emerick, director.

The Center for Creative Living, Athens, Georgia.

Growth centers abound; the list could go on and on. And, increasingly, provisions for study leave and sabbaticals are being written into calls to pastors.

And how are pastors expected to utilize their new skills in base-style churches? The pastor does not have to lead — or even attend — every newly forming small group. His training should have freed him from the compulsive need to control each group. He should, however, be involved in at least one group where he can apply some of his new insights while he himself grows as a person. He can suggest community-building devices for existing groups (such as the session or official board). Many church officers who take time early in a meeting to deal with the "human feelings" and "personal agendas" of participants find themselves better able to deal with issues and make decisions later in the meeting. Giving attention to people affects an overall economy of time.

Lloyd Ogilvie, pastor of the Hollywood Presbyterian Church, considers local church officers the key to the life of the congregation; if a gospel of loving community and relationships is to be proclaimed, the leaders must model it.[4] By developing a

---

[4]Lloyd John Ogilvie, *A Life Full of Surprises* (Nashville: Abingdon Press, 1969), p. 117f.

base community of officers through retreats, luncheons, and small-group meetings, the pastor sets the pace for the entire congregation. Renewal and extended ministries result.

The most significant way that the pastor can apply his new skills is as a trainer of lay leaders for base groups. He has a rare opportunity, for his lay leaders are on the firing line. One pastor meets weekly with his twelve small-group leaders. They themselves become a base community and provide support for the pastor. He, in turn, enables them to report "how it goes" in their groups and provides input which will increase their leadership ability. In some sense, he functions in a "bishop" role with the lay "pastors" of the base groups.

Beyond working with the group leaders, the pastor provides specialty counseling and he visits groups on special occasions (for example, to administer sacraments or to serve as a planning/evaluating consultant). He can help the group write its covenant, then return to evaluate its results. He may also teach seminars and lead retreats for networks of small cells. He usually leads corporate worship when all the groups come together (whether weekly or monthly) for the "big thing." His new enabling skills should especially be operative in the larger assembly, where the service builds upon what the groups bring rather than upon what the lectionary dictates.

2. Ex-Pastors

Works like Laile Bartlett's *The Vanishing Parson* and the United Church of Christ study *Ex-Pastors*, edited by Jerry Jud, document the extent of the clergy dropout phenomenon and the causes. Counseling organizations have been formed to assist professional clergy as they transfer into secular employment. The irony is that it's often the most competent minister who demits. Few of them feel like dropouts — they rather resent the term! They continue to maintain their faith and value system. They still feel they are engaged in ministry, frequently with more satisfying results than when they were in the pastorate. They feel it's the *church* that has dropped out! Too many "Big Daddy" expectations precipitated a crisis of role and identity.

I feel that the exodus and wilderness-wandering of ex-pastors can lead to a promised land. I believe that their talents, faith commitments, and energies can be reclaimed by the church and put to work in new and exciting ways. They can function as "tentmaking" (worker-priest) leaders of base groups. Let me clarify those terms.

The "tentmaking" term grows out of the apostle Paul's experience as a tentmaker in Corinth. He lived with Aquila and Priscilla (Acts 18:3), worked as a tentmaker, and still found time to teach in the synagogue. Later, when churches became strong enough to provide a full or partial financial support, many pastors and evangelists still made their living in a secular occupation. In today's tentmaking ministries, ordained clergymen make their livelihood in the secular world while working in a ministry within or approved by a judicatory. This ministry may be a small congregation, an experimental ministry, or a mission task group.

The term "worker-priest" grew out of the French Catholic clergy's work in secular fields for the expressed purpose of localized ministry. Compensation motivation played second fiddle to ministry motivation. The priest did not plan to gather a community of faith, although he may have operated from a base community. Today, the term "worker-priest" or "worker-minister" describes the clergyman who is secularly employed and whose primary disposition is (1) toward secular work, with a desire to minister in that location, (2) toward building a faith community, with secular employment as a means of livelihood. The latter pattern comes closer to "tentmaking" and describes the role of ex-pastors in base groups. Call them "worker-base ministers."

I believe that any metropolitan area contains numerous ex-pastors who can be recruited, trained, and placed in a supportive network for organizing base groups. One growth strategy for the church could focus upon convening groups around these able people.

Utilization of ex-pastors as conveners would call for training and coordination. An insightful missioner could give full time to training and assembling the network.

Ex-pastors would need to be retrained in enabling skills. Additionally, there should be counseling and group experiences to help the ex-pastor deal with internalized feelings. Some ex-pastors might be ineffective because of unresolved feelings of guilt over going back on a "call" or ordination promise; or because of feelings of inadequacy in failing to cope with the demands of ministry; or of anger directed toward authority figures (church, father, God) or toward laymen for failing to give adequate support. The new group's agenda will be full enough without giving the lion's share of its time to supporting the leaders. Instead, a supportive network of small-group leaders can do that.

The worker-base minister role does not have to be limited to ex-pastors. Small or ineffective congregations are finding it increasingly difficult to pay for building maintenance and a professional staff. An active pastor might secure secular employment; meanwhile, his church could disengage from its building and reshape its life in base groups.

Lowered retirement age plus increased longevity are creating an additional pool of leadership for base communities — provided that the "preach-at-them" style can be avoided. The shell-it-out tendency will tend to fade as more retired ministers gain small-group leadership experience.

Seminarians also might choose to become worker-base ministers. They would obtain secular employment and at the same time convene a faith community around, or in pursuit of, a focused ministry. Many seminaries, recognizing the oversupply of clergy and shifts in occupational patterns, are arranging double-competency curricula in cooperation with nearby universities. A four-year program produces two degrees, one in divinity and a second in law, social work, education, etc.

It is time for established denominations to rethink the ordination patterns of clergy. Is full-time employment as the pastor of a congregation the only requirement for ordination, or can our understanding of ordination to ministry be broadened? A working conference convened by the United Church of Christ and held at La Faret, Colorado, in July, 1971, received proposals on the meaning of ordination from several subgroups. One proposed:

> Ordination is the recognition of special functions that grow out of the general ministry of the church — the functions being those of gathering Christian community and enabling the ministries of others. It is a question of function, not of status. Those people will be ordained who have fulfilled the qualifications to serve those functions of gathering and enabling.

Another group took a more radical stance.

> Ordination as now conceived is inappropriate to emerging ministries. The emerging mission understanding of the church and the crucial nature of ministry in the public sector demand that traditional doctrines of ordination be reformulated along radical lines. In Ephesians 4:1-16, Christian life depends upon participation in community in which all members are gifted by the Holy Spirit with a variety of ministries, in which there are no passengers, and in which status is defined by the reality of functional differentiation. Should not all people committed to Jesus Christ be ordained — or none? To be a serious Christian is to be ordained.[5]

The Southern California Conference of the United Church of Christ developed a worker-base minister model in an effort to reach vast numbers of lonely and alienated persons who are not related to the institutional church. They sought to gather these persons into caring communities. Lay and clergy leaders employed in secular work entered into the following tentmaker ministry covenant.[6]

SOUTHERN CALIFORNIA TENTMAKER MINISTRY COVENANT

PURPOSE

With openness to the abiding presence of the Holy Spirit, in the name of Jesus Christ, we covenant with God in the ministry of gathering together the alienated and unchurched into

[5]Serge F. Hummon, *An Exploration Into Worker Ministries* (New York: United Church Board for Homeland Ministries, Division of Church Extension, 1971), p. 4.

[6]Hummon, Appendix 3.

Christian covenant communities which shall determine their own lifestyle and mission.

GROUP DISCIPLINE

We covenant to meet one Saturday and one weekday evening per month for the purpose of sharing, learning, planning and celebrating (intercessory prayer, sacramental life, personal study, continuous evaluation).

We affirm that absolute honesty, trust and openness to criticism are essential to the health of our community and we pledge to support one another, individually and corporately, whenever that support is needed and requested.

SPECIALIZED TRAINING

We covenant to contract with COMMIT for specialized training and process consultation. In addition, we shall avail ourselves of other resources as required.

ACCOUNTABILITY

We covenant to be responsible to God and conscience and accountable to the Church Extension and Nurture Commission of the Southern California Conference of the United Church of Christ through its staff liaison. Furthermore, we shall share, on a regular basis, our experiences and insights with the wider fellowship.

LENGTH OF COMMITMENT AND MAXIMUM SIZE

We covenant to participate fully in this community for a period of two years, terminating in June, 1973.

This community shall be limited to a maximum of twelve persons.

RE-NEGOTIATION

We covenant to review and/or re-negotiate this covenant every three months or upon the request of any member of the community.

3. The Laity

I insist that the promotion of base communities is *not* an attempt to eliminate professional leadership from the church, nor to open the floodgates to untrained leadership. Having said that, I want to move on to affirm that the vitality of the base group will depend upon the competence of good lay leadership. To some extent, leadership in the group will be shared by all, yet in every group a few natural leaders emerge. The Bell and Howell *Encountertapes* propose leaderless groups, but even here someone has to say "Let's begin" and turn on the tape recorder. Leaderless groups do not exist! Let's acknowledge that fact and build base communities on the selection and training of good leaders.

Utilizing lay leaders in base groups will threaten many clergymen — shifts in power and control always threaten. But our present clergy-dominated structures are not the answer either. For example, our church traditions tend to mitigate against lay preaching out of fears that heresy, incompetence, and ignorance would spread. Untrained and ignorant persons might dilute the gospel and turn it into folk religion! The 1970's, however, present a different picture from yesteryear. A higher educational level across the board places effective lay training in theology and group process within reach of millions of laymen. Most pastors have one or more parishioners with more years of formal education than they themselves have.

Moreover, indigenous lay leadership has unique value for the ministering process within the small group. John Wesley recognized this when he forbade preachers to be leaders of the class meetings. He instructed that the "most insignificant" person in each class be the leader of it.

Our professional patterns take a leader out of the congregation; we then send him away to seminary where he obtains a new vocabulary and joins an elitist group. He forfeits his amateur status and in some way grows out of touch with his fellows. Is it unreasonable to suggest that the base group might recognize the gifts and call of a person to be their leader and representative without sending him away to school? The missionary movement suffered because indigenous leadership was not utilized. Leadership resided in paid professionals whose academic and cultural credentials were set by the countries from whence they came. The New Testament pattern placed the ministry of new congregations in the hands of indigenous leaders, even the ministry of the Word and sacraments. The community recognized its natural leaders. Educational attainments or professional status had only incidental bearing upon their selection. Fortunately, mission strategists are returning to this concept.

John Tanburn, in *Open House*, tells his house church experience. He suggests that the minister of a congregation should function as a bishop to the house church cells, and that each group should have an ordained lay pastor functioning as its leader for a limited time (one year). In this way, the congregation would not be structured around, or be dependent upon, one man.

Perhaps the failure of the mainline, white denominations to recruit minorities — poor, ethnic, and racial — exposes our inability to utilize indigenous leadership at the grass-roots level. The base-style church offers the setting for recovering indigenous leadership.

Christians in Asia, Africa, and Latin America have much to teach us. In Asia and Africa, one ordained, full-time minister is in charge of twenty to sixty village congregations. In some parts of South India, limitations of sacramental and pastoral services have encouraged the training and ordination of lay leaders. The seminaries have cooperated in establishing a three-year "in-service" training program. Three weeks per year are spent at the seminary in intensive training, followed by year-round tutoring classes led by an area presbyter. The class agenda grows out of their daily ministering experience. Students maintain their secular jobs and God blesses the church! In twelve years, the number of village congregations has quadrupled. The church was willing to recognize and build upon the ministry of those whom the Holy Spirit was using as apostles, even though they had little education. At the same time, we should also note that the work could never have been accomplished without full-time, well-trained presbyters, professors, and bishops.

In Latin America, the rapid expansion of the Pentecostal churches underlines the possibilities for utilizing indigenous lay leadership. In Pentecostal services, all persons are permitted full participation in worship, testimony, and service. As one's gifts are developed and recognized by the church, he is given additional leadership responsibility. In-service apprenticeship becomes the training vehicle for volunteer leaders. They become full-time leaders when they reach maturity. The flexible patterns of ministry generate an intense sense of belonging and provide the basis for a powerful evangelistic appeal.[7]

Why can't these insights be appropriated in our western world? In a day when only 8 percent of the American population attends church on any given Sunday, surely the possibilities for missionary activity exist. The strategy for church growth through the multiplication of base cells calls for competent and indigenous lay leadership to function at the heart of the movement.

Lay leadership training may be approached in either of two ways. One method is to convene a group and allow the natural leaders to rise to the top, like cream. These identified leaders can then be given specialized training outside the group. The other route is to select potential leaders for intensive training and then have them, either singly or in pairs, convene a group around them. In either case, training must include (1) heavy "front end" orientation for launching base groups, and (2) continual "in-service" feedback and updating with a support group.

Lay training can take place in the parish, in lay-training centers, and in seminaries. All three locations are crucial areas for increased activity; however, the trainers must be motivated to deal with the real agenda of the laity rather than imposing a prescribed agenda.

The base for decision-making needs to be broadened to include greater lay participation, and the restructuring into base groups can provide that broader base. Many denominations are wrestling with changes in lay participation in decision-making. Could base-group leaders participate in the administrative system and also be permitted to administer Word and sacrament? I think we need to move in those directions. In the meantime, we do not have to wait until the rules are changed to initiate base communities. In the Presbyterian order, for instance, the body of ruling elders (who are ordained) could be leaders of base

7Hummon, pp. 6-7.

communities and function in administrative roles. Regulations already allow more freedom than we are exercising.

John Tanburn concludes his appeal for the Church of England to permit short-term, functional ordination of lay pastors for house churches:

> What is needed is a form of ministry that not only ensures the unity and continuity of the church in space and time, but also allows the local church freedom to structure its life organically in relation to its particular needs, and in relation to the distinctive gifts of its individual members. The meeting of local needs will necessitate the power to ordain real lay pastors having authority to minister the Word and Sacraments in their local churches just as validly as our present clergy; gifted individuals urgently require an enhanced diaconate, national and local.
>
> It is imperative that the theologians urgently work out a ministerial structure that reflects the church's organic nature and forwards its mission-servant role, to replace the world-style monolithic top-down power structures that we are so prone to; an ecclesiastical polity that is not an end in itself, but based on the sole purpose of forwarding the life and mission of the church at every level, especially the truly local. Such structures must urgently be evolved and continually reassessed both locally and nationally. In neither case is it actually impossible; and in neither case will the church be seen to be the church of Christ until it is done.[8]

What To Train Them For

Following the House Church Consultation at Louisville Seminary in November, 1971, I met with a caucus of Presbyterian participants. All were practicing leaders of house churches. I asked these questions: "Where do we go from here? What is the next thing for us to do?"

They wanted to (1) participate in a communication network, and (2) receive training for themselves and for their other leaders. Many house church models were represented at the consultation, each one having a unique slant. Some were strong

[8]John Tanburn, *Open House* (London: Falcon Books, 1970), p. 97.

on the human-potential movement, some on mission action, and some on communalism. Our caucus saw value in each, but we were reluctant to single out any one style as the model for training. We suggested that a training model should be developed which would synthesize the best elements, including insights into celebration, charismatic experience, intergenerational learning, small-group process, "body life" communalism, and mission action.

The suggestions of the consultation participants provide guidelines for outlining an effective training program for both clergy and lay base-group leaders. Each trainee could be evaluated in six skill areas, and appropriate training programs would be negotiated. The six skills are:

1. Celebration

Liturgical renewal is the "in thing" for the 70's. The reams of mimeographed contemporary worship materials floating around attest that liturgical renewal is a "movement." No one has written the complete handbook yet, thank God. New ways keep surfacing.

Many of our traditional worship patterns are celebrations based upon Isaiah's experience in the temple (Isaiah 6) where he saw the Lord "lifted up." Then Isaiah saw himself as unclean, and he received mercy and healing. Finally, he heard the call, "go," and he offered himself: "Here I am." That one Biblical account has become the norm, but think of the possibilities for using other orders, of celebrating other passages of scripture. We can get our feelings inside the experiences of Jesus, or inside the struggles of his disciples, or inside the adventures of the infant church. Our grounding (identity as God's people) needs to find expression. Celebration skills help a base group to locate their experiences, connect them to the insights of the biblical tradition, and lift them to God in prayer and praise.

2. Group Process

This book was not written to serve as a handbook for group process. (The whole volume would be taken up with small-group theory and practice.) Much good information is available — so much that the overexposed small-group leader may feel overwhelmed by it all. Trying to take it all in is like drinking from a fire hose!

The National Training Labs in Washington, D. C., make available excellent training programs and materials. A helpful set of small-group aids is a series of three structured booklets on human-relations training by William Pfeiffer and John E. Jones. Their latest undertaking is the *1972 Annual Handbook for Group Facilitators*.[9] In the Lay Renewal stream, the Serendipity series published by Lyman Coleman provides excellent tools for leaders with limited experience. Tape resources are also available. Forum House Publishers has released a nine-session series of structured experiences in personal growth and engagement in ministry entitled "The Church in Small Groups."[10] The cassette outlines minimal structure requirements for the group and offers tips for leaders.

The novice leader can begin to "build a bag" of procedures and experiences. Apprenticing with an established group leader affords him the opportunity to observe the behavioral effect which certain structures provoke in the group. He selects those methods which he finds legitimate and helpful. Being confident and comfortable with his own bag rather than borrowing someone else's will make him a more effective leader. Small-group "gimmicks" can dig up more snakes than inexperienced leaders can kill! On the other hand, if the leader provides no structure at all, the group will wallow in the quagmire of nondirection.

Let's look at some of the specific skills which a small group leader will use. The list is certainly not exhaustive. It is only suggestive.

(1) Contracting. Some groups never get off the ground because the goals and expectations of the individual members are too diverse for the group to work in concert. The health of any organization is usually determined by a clear statement of understanding and an agreed-upon method for pursuing goals.

[9]University Associates, Post Office Box 615, Iowa City, Iowa 52240.

[10]Forum House Publishers, 1610 LaVista Road, Northeast, Atlanta, Georgia 30329.

The small-group leader begins by helping the group to form a contract: What is the purpose of the group? To what disciplines or tasks will each participating member commit himself? The leader will help the group to differentiate between maintenance goals and task goals and will help the group to evaluate its contract and negotiate a new one, if this is indicated.

(2) Communicating. People communicate in many ways, overt and subtle. The most obvious medium is conversation. The leader can notice which person talks, for how long, how often, and to whom the talk is directed. Assertions, questions, and tone of voice give clues to what is going on in the group and reveal who leads and influences.

People also communicate through "body language." Gestures and unintentional signs — for example, sitting posture and even the position of the chair itself — indicate whether a person is "in" the group or has "checked out."

When the leader "reads" either word language or body language and recognizes feelings of fear, anger, pain, boredom, or excitement, he is in a position to assist healthy communication flow. He may choose to call a spade a spade, identifying the emotion and getting it out on the table. Given a friendly climate, people can learn that they don't have to fear their emotions; they can openly state, "I feel angry," etc. The here-and-now expression of feelings (contrasted to the then-and-there report) brings the total person into the group in a direct way so that he can be "heard."

The leader serves the group by clarifying and summarizing what has been offered and testing to see how it has been received. Active listening can be improved by the total group as well as by the leader. Very soon the group will pick up the leader's techniques and will test their own listening ability through a process of restating, clarifying, and summarizing.

(3) Trusting. Building a community of good will on the basis of mutual trust is foundational to every other aspect of group development. The leader can facilitate acceptance by finding ways to acknowledge persons, whether he does this through facial expressions or overt statements. He can help the group to make similar responses.

Check to see if the group is responding to persons as they share. Don't let the person go away feeling lonely or estranged. Ask, "Did we leave (name of person) hanging in the air?"

An authoritarian stance places the group leader in a precarious position because it encourages people to ask direct questions and ask for advice. This is a trap, often leading to oversimplified answers, and it will be copied by participants. "Dime store" analysis and evaluations will discourage participants from sharing for fear their offerings will be torn to shreds. A more helpful posture is simply to be with another person in his search and struggle. Stay alongside the person and his feelings, rather than short-circuiting the trusting process with a full explanation and full set of instructions. Sometimes a direct answer is called for, but blessed is he who has been delivered from the compulsion of offering an analysis or answer for every situation and problem!

Robert Leslie suggests that the best way to build trust is for the leader to be trusting. The three basic qualities which he identifies are empathy, warmth, and genuineness.[11] With these qualities operative, along with the ability to free the group to be responsible for itself, trust will grow and deepen.

(4) Modeling. The group rarely rises above its leader, for one of the sharpest teaching devices in experimental learning is modeling. A leader who risks to share his feelings will enable the group to be real with one another. A leader who is willing to play a hunch teaches participants to learn to trust their own intuitions. A leader who becomes vulnerable by exposing his own weakness communicates an invaluable lesson in mutually shared ministry. Falling on one's face in failure is no fun, but running the risk affords growth for the leader and sets the tone for the cellular base group.

(5) Resolving. Unresolved conflicts impede the growth and effectiveness of the church. Conflict has been a "no-no." Feelings get swept under the rug for the sake of "unity,"

[11]Robert Leslie, *Sharing Groups in the Church* (Nashville: Abingdon Press, 1971), p. 182.

"purpose," and "love," but to avoid conflict is to avoid the possibilities for growth and development. Married couples frequently look back upon their experiences in resolving conflict as a growth period in their relationship. Church people and institutions need to see that unresolved conflict destroys, while resolved conflict is creative. If the trainer knows his own inner conflicts and resolves them, he can begin to assist others in the resolution of interpersonal conflicts.

One reason the authoritarian leadership model has been able to survive and prosper in the church is that people have not been able to risk openly stating their own goals, hopes, and dreams. To do this would place them in conflict with other persons who have differing goals. Rather than working these conflicts out in a way in which all could learn and grow together, they have opted out and fallen in line behind the goals of the authoritarian leader. But in the base community, the enabling leader can help people to understand and accept their real goals and values. They can explore both shared and divergent aspirations. If conflicts continue to fester, the whole group will pay the price in lack of communication and trust.

(6) Deciding. Decision-making can be fostered by the leader who helps the group to get adequate information. A wealth of information can be drawn from throughout the group if the group will glean this information from everyone rather than from the dominant few. Once the information emerges, the leader can encourage clear decision-making, whether by polling the group, voting or testing for consensus. Often groups ramble on and on, wasting valuable time, when a decision has already been made. (They were not conscious of it.) Sending up trial balloons can keep the group on track, alert to what decision it is they are wrestling with, bringing them to a point of decision, or confirming that a decision has already been made.

3. Intergenerational Nurture

In church activities, we are so accustomed to being divided along age, peer-group, or sex lines that we have failed to recognize and develop the rich potential for intergenerational small-group experience. In conversations about house churches, the question of "What do you do with the children?" always arises. No conclusive answer is possible, for the house church does not have a long "track record." Signs emerge, however, that inter-generational learning is feasible. Family camp and conference ministries have gained some insights, as have family lab experiments within the human potential movement. The development of resource materials as well as continued experimentation is a must. We are not serving the nuclear family well with our stratified approach.

My family and I engaged in a nine-month experiment of intergenerational nurture and worship. We gathered every Sunday evening around a low, improvised table. Adults and children sat together on the floor, eating finger foods off the table. A theme expressed in a single word provided direction for all of the activities, which included singing, bread-breaking, praying, dancing, role playing, and any other structure through which we could express and affirm some aspect of our faith. The inter-generational relationships which were built created an extended-family atmosphere which had meaning for both children and adults. (See Appendix B.)

4. Theological Reflection

Someone has said that the effective preacher is one who holds the Bible in one hand and the newspaper in the other. He discerns what is going on in the world, as well as how God has acted through his people in the course of history. The process of theologizing, or "doing theology," connects the person to his religious heritage and to the contemporary call of God in the world.

The church has suffered from its failure to do its theological task. We grasp at straws and look for new winds to blow more straws down the road from the secular world. We can learn from the world while, at the same time, drawing upon our heritage. The skill of relating the real-life, present situation to the biblical Word does not belong to the "preacher" alone, but must be shared by the laity in the context of the life of the base community.

5. Mission Action

The church's seeming inability to reach out in ministry to the world through the congregational form will not be resolved by simply changing that form or chopping the congregation into smaller units. The costly grace of discipleship is less appealing than the cheap grace of having one's needs met. The slow and tedious process of enabling a group to engage in ministry outside itself must be attempted if the base church is going to have integrity.

The Rev. Don Allen, pastor of Trinity Presbyterian Church in Harrisonburg, Virginia, keeps the mission call in high visibility before the house churches within his congregation. He lists six skills which a mission leader should fulfill within the house church. They are:

(1)   The mission leader should possess theological maturity concerning the mission of the church in the world.

(2)   The mission leader needs to be acquainted with and sensitive to the issues, hurts, and needs in the local community.

(3)   Skill is needed to relate the discovered community needs, etc., to the empathetic hurts and capabilities of the members of the group.

(4)   Base group facilitating skills are necessary to enable the group to function with as much "health" as possible in moving toward their chosen tasks.

(5)   The mission leader needs an acquaintance with goal-setting skills to make specific the steps taken in mission development.

(6)   The mission leader should continually relate the specific activities in which the house church is engaged to the overarching evangelistic purposes and theological perspectives.[12]

6. Planning

The nuts-and-bolts process of planning, which embraces goal setting, decision making, and evaluation has been treated elsewhere in this book. I would simply underline the importance of

[12]Donald Allen, *Suggested Qualities and Skills Necessary for an Effective Mission Leader of a House Church* (unpublished pamphlet), p. 1.

helping people to locate their dreams. The church is guilty of not thinking big enough. God implants big dreams. Exercising imagination and engaging in fantasy can move the group off dead center. One wise group leader put it this way: "What would you do today both as an individual and as a group if you knew you couldn't fail?" Once the dream has been seen and stated, the group can respond with its own gifts and will move toward that vision.

Church groups need more Don Quixotes who can dream the impossible dream. The role of the leader is to help put wheels under the dream.

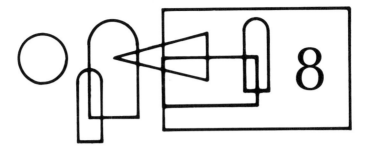

8

SHIFTING GEARS

> Regularly, but perhaps not always on Sundays, members of those congregations will gather in some common place. And when they gather they will share their deepest concerns with each other and with God. They will explore the Scriptures and perhaps sing a song or two. Someone will probably preach from the Scriptures. Then they will gather around a table of some kind, and someone will bring a loaf of bread and a bottle of wine . . . . It is to that far country that our congregations are on their exodus.[1]

The "exodus" to which Loren Mead refers is a precarious one. Any change in the church stirs mixed reactions. The house church will be regarded as a blessing by some, a curse by others.

I have suggested that an impersonal, success-oriented, edifice-centered, and clergy-dominated congregational model of Christian community constricts the creative possibilities in the church. I have suggested that building church structures upon a network of interdependent, small, base groups is vital to the renewal of the church, and that the new forms may be constructed within, alongside, or outside the parish congregation. I envision the church in the "promised land" functioning with diverse cells, all bearing the full marks of the church. This church operates within every conceivable stream of society, and it eagerly faces the future.

Meanwhile, the exodus — the wilderness journeying — will

[1] Loren B. Mead, *New Hope for Congregations* (New York: Seabury Press, 1972), p. 128.

evoke false starts, turning back, misunderstanding, and weariness. However, the restlessness over the present and the vision for the future will insure the continuation of the journey. With many restraining forces operating, these days of transition call for clear and intentional strategies; without strategies, we will either die in the wilderness or return to bondage in Egypt.

For contemporary man, change is a norm. Change is all about us. It affects every institution of society, and the church is not exempt. A stable social or ecclesiastical environment produces a seeming security, with predictable behavior; but when the world shifts, the church feels the tremor. The church can either strike out to meet the world or remove itself to a secure cove where disturbing waves from rocking boats can no longer be felt. In either case, the church has changed. Change is unavoidable — the real question is, "How will we change?"

The church does not need to fear change — unless its real commitments are to the idols of security. God's movement in the church has always been one of change in pursuit of a kingdom where love, justice, and righteousness will exist, and where people will live in community.

A pastor-friend recalled the fear which change imposed on his people. He decided to study in depth the dynamics of change. Suddenly, he realized that change was the church's business. The Holy Spirit is the agent of change; repentance and growth are the language of change. He then began to lead his people into an understanding of the dynamics of personal and corporate change. All renewalists need this understanding.

The changing times force people into change, and they need growing space and a supportive structure in which to discover more of their God-given gifts and capacities. The director of a crisis-intervention ministry for youth commented, "As I move around, I don't see any congregations which really are effectively helping people grow and change. Finding the form and structures in which people can grow becomes an imperative for the church."

A research study conducted by the Synod of Texas, "Why People Join the Presbyterian Church, U.S.," revealed that "virtually all the new members, in describing the circumstances under which they first began thinking of joining, talk about circumstances that involve some major change in their personal situation — marriage, geographical move, vocational change, illness, death, birth of children, going away from home to college or service. The implication is that at such a time a person is most likely to be open to an invitation to consider church membership."[2]

If people are more open to the church when they are in the midst of change, then situational groupings of small numbers of persons in base communities can become a powerful and appropriate evangelism tactic. We can help people with shared change factors to group for common support and growth, following the Alcoholics Anonymous pattern.

Someone has said that the seven last words of the church are, "We never did it that way before!" True, people need tradition — a history, a story. However, we must enable them to understand that the real tradition — the community which Jesus constructed and which the early church modeled — contains the dynamics of change. If people can assess the changing world in terms of our authentic tradition, constructive change is possible. New Christian forms will appear as the Spirit births a variety of new communities of faith and action. Moving into these strange structures will require risky choices.

Transitional strategies must be developed within the *church* but beyond the *edifice*. Theological integrity and able leadership are the materials.

Within the Church

I do not want to start a new denomination or an anti-institutional underground church. I do propose a transition within existing church structures to expand the options for Christian community.

We have seen the death of groups in the so-called underground. Hundreds of them disappeared within a year or two of

[2]"Why People Join The Presbyterian Church, U.S." (Austin, Texas: Synod of Texas, 1968), p. 21.

their formation. Rootlessness and lack of connection hastened their demise. These groups needed the trained leadership and adequate resources which only a larger connectional framework can dependably provide.

Paul likened the church to a body. Life can be found in the cell, but the cells must live in connection, never alone! Vilmos Vajto, director of the Ecumenical Research Centre in Strasbourg, reinforces this concept. He suggests that modern society has challenged the traditional structures of the Christian community, exposing the need for new patterns in which personal relationships are possible. "A personalized community life of this kind must be conceived of in terms of small units. This mini-church would be worthless unless it regarded its communion with the universal church as a fundamental importance."[3]

Those who have worked with ongoing groups raise the question, "How long can (or should) a group continue — eight weeks, one year, five years, twenty years?" If groups have a limited life span and then die, who will conduct the funeral? What will happen to the surviving people? Unless the groups are connected to a congregation, network, or judicatory with oversight and support responsibilities, the people will get lost. The "system" can function to help them into and out of a variety of groups.

The newly forming base communities must recognize that the total church system is interdependent. What happens in one part of the system will affect the other parts. Experimental groups on the fringe of the church find it difficult to sustain life and become self-supporting. (But even if their life span is short and even if they seemingly fail, the mainstream church will nonetheless be richer because of their explorations.)

The church is called to be creative and to build institutions which can make an effective witness appropriate to our time. Here history has something to teach us. The Sunday School movement began when evangelism and teaching opportunities among children were ripe. Church-related colleges began dotting the frontier when church expansion increased the need for

[3]"Jesus: Solution or Salvation," *This Month* (November, 1972), p. 9.

educated Christian leadership. Churches built children's homes in the South on the heels of the Civil War to care for thousands of homeless children. All of these institutions were built in response to the needs of a given period.

Our day is characterized by loneliness, impersonalism, and a need to belong and contribute. Again, new institutions must be built to meet prevailing needs.

The new institutions suggested here are base communities, with decentralization of the decision-making process. The church cannot afford the clergy-laity gap. Laymen must be permitted to deal with the issues if they are expected to support the church's programs. We also need clear authority-accountability lines. Differences and conflicts will arise within and between base groups. The groups will be most healthy when communication lines and decision lines are clear. I see a nightmare if thousands of maverick groups spontaneously do their own thing without having to answer to any brother for their conduct!

Many of the new interdependent base communities will be ecumenical. Denominations provide connection, but metropolitan social patterns do not "jive" with denominational nuances. New ecumenical congregations and clusters of churches of different denominations can help to gear the church for mission if denominations do not insist upon superimposing their own requirements. Such imposition can push the cooperating costs too high, and new ecumenical communities must operate on lean budgets.

The new institutional styles must also be capable of embracing diversity. Pluralism is the new name of the game. Historically, the Roman Catholics have shown more wisdom here than the Protestants. Recognizing that many missions require gifts, abilities, and commitments which are not found within a local parish, the Catholics established orders — gathered communities called to perform specialized ministries.

It would be folly for me to suggest that all church people should immediately move into house churches. Many do not choose to, nor are they ready for such a move.

But inside and outside the church, people are available to

form a nucleus, and leadership is emerging. We can build a variety of models. The transition will be achieved, then, through the movement of people who are ready to go, rather than through an edict.

Beyond the Edifice

The early Christian church got along okay for three centuries without buildings, but a quick count of church spires reveals that buildings are highly valued today. People rarely picture "church" without seeing a "place."

In most cities, downtown and midtown churches are suffering attrition of members. Dwindling membership rolls leave the churches with empty space, even on Sunday. They try to find ways to utilize their space during the week but rarely succeed. Building maintenance costs compete with program and mission needs.

The midtown suburbs (those built 15 to 25 years ago) contain churches which once experienced rapid growth but now have dwindling attendance, even though the roll remains constant. The mortgage on the last building unit has just been paid. Hostility, previously subdued in order to project a "unified front," begins to surface, and people raise the question, "What is our purpose and goal, anyway?"

The mid-range suburbs contain churches galore. In one southern city, I saw four new, small churches on each of several intersections. All were struggling to pay for programs and buildings out of memberships under 200. They have undertaken tremendous building debts on the basis of overoptimistic membership projections.

The more recently developing outer suburbs show reduced church construction. Denominational agencies have gained insight and are trying to avoid past mistakes. Smaller multi-purpose units now dot the landscape. Still, their progressive-minded young families harbor hopes of recreating a building which will look like the old home-church and will afford the security that the old church provided. If the new church becomes successful, it can grow. Ultimately, it can build the cathedral of everyone's dreams — and spend the next twenty years paying for it!

The real cost of overbuilding is not only in dollars, but also in misplaced focus of life and mission — a focus upon a particular time and particular place.

My critics object, saying people need a "place" and that our buildings provide a symbolic identity and an emotional security framework. I realize that places occupy a significant role in people's lives — especially places of decision, tragedy, and celebration. People cherish places where baptism, marriage, and funerals can be held, surrounded by Christian symbols and bathed in the soft glow of tradition. I acknowledge the value of this assertion. At the same time, however, I would observe that "peak" religious experiences happen not only in the sanctuary, but also in intimate small groupings and even in times of aloneness. We are still reaping the whirlwind of the medieval belief that God was offered through the Mass — a peak religious event which was enclosed in a church building.

I would say that people do not need a religious *place* so much as they need a religious *experience*. They need to express symbolically their *own* celebration experiences, meanwhile tying their symbols to the tradition. Some house churches have constructed their own symbols in banners and other portable objects. These provide an identifiable environment for each gathering as the base group moves from place to place. The groups surround themselves with accounts of their Christian pilgrimage. A parallel can be seen in the Israelites, who wandered in the wilderness as a tent people, carrying their religious symbols with them.

The church's utter dependence upon a place reveals an adolescent behavior pattern. When the church comes to a mature understanding of the gospel, valuing life together and mission to the world, it can be weaned from this dependency. Then the edifice complex will no longer rob the church of its vital energy and resources.

Having said this, I would hasten to add that although the church is not dependent upon a special "place," it does need "space." Some of this space will be in church buildings. We do not, however, need church buildings in the number and of the type that now exist. The following options can be considered:

1. Where feasible, meet in homes — especially in extended-family, household base groups.

2. Utilize public space — parks, schools, apartment house social rooms, etc.

3. Rent space in restaurants, movie theaters, banks, shopping centers, etc.

4. Reduce church construction to a minimum, building only multiple-use space.

5. Share facilities with other congregations through cooperative scheduling.

6. Cluster congregations to facilitate sharing of existing buildings. Unused buildings can be rented or sold.

7. Remodel existing space for more versatility. Most church sanctuaries are so rigid that they demand authoritarian performances; they preempt options for innovative worship, teaching, and programs. Nearly 2,000 of the 4,000 congregations of the Presbyterian Church, U.S., have fewer than 100 members; yet, they are trying to function by the cathedral model. If they could appropriate new leadership styles, remodel and rearrange their sanctuaries (claiming their smallness as power, rather than feeling guilty and inadequate because they do not grow), a host of participatory base communities would be "born again."

8. Sell the edifice and reconstitute the church into house groups.

9. Identify and make full use of several large, cathedral-type churches.

I have repeatedly affirmed the need and value of both the intimate house church and the mass cathedral experience. If we could make full use of large buildings (cathedrals) and free the smaller groups to meet informally in homes or public places, we could gear down our almost compulsive church construction system.

With Theological Integrity

Any attempt to organize alternate forms of Christian community on the basis of "we are all good fellows who can benefit by sticking together" will self-destruct. If history teaches us anything, it teaches us the inherent bankruptcy of attempts to build human community on inadequate or misplaced goals.

The human-potential movement has opened vast horizons for understanding human growth and interpersonal relationships, and the church can gain immensely by appropriating these new insights. But the church also has its own dimensions of life — for instance, reservoirs of experience and tradition which cannot be ignored or discounted. Affirmations of the transcendent cannot be tossed out the window. Doing theological reflection becomes imperative.

Maintaining theological integrity means paying attention to these three principles:

1. The human dilemma destroys community. Man's "inhumanity to man," his will to power, his self-centeredness, his insensitivity to needs are negative tendencies which must be acknowledged. Without facing them, the movement would become another utopian dream certain to be shattered.

2. True community is God's gift. Jesus Christ breaks down dividing walls. The Holy Spirit authors unity. Acknowledging the transcendent dimensions of life glues the community together. The church is *more than* a gathering of people — how else could we explain the very existence of the church after 2,000 chaotic years?

3. Community propels the church outward into mission. The church exists as God's instrument for the world. A kingdom is emerging; a world is being built upon God's love, justice, and righteousness.

The sources for theologizing are available. Scripture, creeds, history, and experience can give clergy and laity direction. Christians can move boldly when they possess and act out of conviction and authority.

Peter Berger suggested as much in his comments to the Denver meeting of COCU in 1971.

> I would also affirm that the concern for the institutional structures of the church will be vain unless there is also a new conviction and a new authority in the Christian community. There will almost certainly have to be structural changes (though, I suspect, they will in the end turn out to be less

drastic than many now hope or fear). There will have to be sustained thought as to the proper response of Christians to the agonizing travail of American society. However, it seems to me that these tasks will be meaningful only to the extent that the Christian community regains its "nerve" and succeeds in achieving a new stance of confidence in itself and its message.[4]

Doctrine is not the only organizing principle for church structures. For leaders on the western frontier, the difference between failure and success was conditioned by their ability to organize around the character and needs of the settlers rather than around doctrinal principles exclusively.

Effective organization places *both* the theological tradition and the contemporary situation into the mold.

By Able Leadership

No attempt at church renewal will rise above a leadership which is unwilling to risk. The total church system must open up new options. The house-church leader cannot do it all by himself, as pivotal as his position might be.

Let's eavesdrop on a series of conversations between an advocate of base groups, on the one hand, and certain "church folk," on the other.

Between an advocate and a denominational executive.

ADVOCATE: How does it feel up there?

DENOMINATIONAL EXECUTIVE: It's not what it used to be.

A.   How so?

DE. Well, we used to create a lot of programs, manage large budgets, and were well thought of in the church. But lately, few people trust us — only about 30 percent of our constituency. The money tree is drying up. Our staffs have been drastically reduced and agency-restructuring activity has us up in the air.

[4]Peter Berger, "A Call for Authority in Christian Community," *Christian Century* (October 27, 1971), p. 1263.

A.　So, what does all of this mean? How does it affect the renewal concerns which I am bringing to you?

DE.　Don't get your hopes up. The church grows weary of new schemes. We've tried new programs, and few have paid off. We have less and less power to affect the grass roots from our position in the superstructure. Besides, we tried your house-church thing in the 50's and it didn't work. Over the years, they failed to grow. What makes you think they could thrive now?

A.　The house churches of the 50's still depended upon authoritarian leadership. Then, in the 60's they leaned toward social activism as the organizing principle. But today, it's a new ball game. Look at the decay of congregational life, and the loneliness and alienation that prevail in the world. We've learned a lot about group dynamics, which can make a difference in the 70's.

DE.　We are really more open to the house church than you may think — experimentation consumes a large hunk of our time and mission money. You show us that new base forms have validity and vitality and we will be on your side!

A.　But are you willing to move over?

DE.　Move over?

A.　Yes. You said you've lost "power," and I think I noticed a trace of regret in your voice. We are talking about laying a base for the church in which laymen will share power, participating in decision-making all the way up, even into the superstructure.

DE.　That's okay with me. Too much has been controlled from here anyway. Our expenditures and programs don't always match the commitment of grass-roots people. Besides, we tend to operate from secure and safe positions too much of the time. We need to be pushed into risky areas.

A.　I'm glad to hear that. Let me suggest some ways you can help. First, take a new look at both lay and clergy ordination. Second, nudge the seminaries to go into lay training. Third, publicize churches that are moving onto base, and plant some seeds in mission-strategy committees. You may be riding a wild horse before you know it!

Between an advocate and a judicatory executive.

ADVOCATE: What's new with you?

JUDICATORY EXECUTIVE: I'm feeling my oats!

A.   That you are! I hear you are a new breed of cat! I used to know you guys as the cautious old guard. Now you are younger, more aware, alive. What happened?

JE. Well, our offices used to be manned by former successful pastors; they were appointed to these executive positions in reward for years of pastoral service. But all of that has been changing. Church organizational behavior has become a science, and we have been trained as specialists in this field. Management is our forte. We see the church as a system and try to involve as many gifted people as possible in its efforts.

A.   Even laymen?

JE. *Especially* laymen — and *laywomen*! Lay persons are the hope of the church.

A.   Can the house church fit into your system?

JE. That depends. Many people are not ready for it. Tall-steeple pastors are threatened by it. Our mission committees still tend to see church development as building churches in outlying areas. But I am personally open, and I have hope. We need to see working models. What do you suggest?

A.   Give me the names of a few pastors who are open to small, innovative groups; the names of some ex-pastors who would like to work; some active laymen, and some lay dropouts. I would like to share my own vision with them and introduce them to other house-church practitioners. After we have explored together various possibilities, we would like to talk to your mission committee!

Between an advocate and a pastor.

ADVOCATE: Have you ever heard of the house church?

PASTOR: Sounds like competition to me!

A.   Well, it could be, but it doesn't have to be. Many house churches exist within congregations.

P.   You must be talking about *small groups*. We have had some good ones. People who like them seem to come alive and grow. I'm all for them, but I have to admit I've been frustrated. They seem to spurt, then wind down, and finally stop. I don't understand why.

A.   The house church is a small group, but it's much more, for it carries more freight. It embraces worship, fellowship, nurture, and action. Strong church support and leadership is a must if a base church is to get off the ground.

P.   I would really like to see this church turned upside down through house churches. I'd be willing to let all the traditional programs go, with the exception of the eleven o'clock worship hour — and maybe that, too, on occasion. But I don't know how. Where do I begin?

A.   Certainly not by arbitrarily halting all church programming. Begin by expanding your own leadership "bag" in the direction of an enabling style. Get additional training in small-group methodology and the development of voluntary organizations. Try out your new leadership insights in existing groups, in new house churches, or even in corporate worship. This will be a "seeding" process aimed at freeing up your people. New structures take form around "life." Expose your laymen to good training — perhaps you would like to train them yourself. Let them see models of house churches. Inculcate an understanding of the dynamics of change.

P.   This sounds exciting — but scary.

A.   Scary?

P.   Yes, I see a lot of personal risk. People want to be told what to do. They want me to lead and support them.

A.   But *you* need support too!

P.   Exactly, but can I acknowledge this need and still ask
     people for their support?

A.   The new style of ministry is a two-way street! You need a
     support group within the church. You also need support
     from other pastors who are in the same boat. Let me
     suggest some names to you . . . .

Between an advocate and an ex-pastor.

ADVOCATE: Where are you in your church experience now?

EX-PASTOR: I'm neither fish nor fowl. Since I left the parish,
     we've been shopping around for a church. Wherever I go, I
     have an uneasy feeling. I'm not a pastor to the congrega-
     tion, yet I don't feel like a layman, either. The members
     expect more of me, and the pastor keeps a cautious eye
     on me.

A.   How do you feel about the church?

EP. I have had mixed feelings. I'm still angry at the church for
     what happened to me and my family — we were expected
     to fill roles which wouldn't allow us to be ourselves. I've
     tried to resolve this resentment. Sometimes I feel a twinge
     of guilt over leaving. After all, as a sixteen-year-old, I
     dedicated my "whole life" to the ministry. But on the
     whole, I have good feelings about the Christian faith, if
     not about the church as I experienced it. In many ways, I
     think I'm doing a more effective ministry now as a layman!

A.   In what way?

EP. Well, I've become a real person, I'm more relaxed, less
     defensive, and I have a new sense of power. People take
     me for what I am.

A.   Will you ever return to the pastorate?

EP. Definitely not! I couldn't afford to financially. Besides, I
     could never return to that role. I would have to move into
     a church structure that is small and personal, with very
     little "order" and a lot of love.

A.   I know just the place!

EP.   You do?

A.   Yes, a house church, a base church.

EP.   Do you mean an underground thing?

A.   No. I mean a small church above ground. A house church develops its own worship and work life, but it's connected to a network of several other base groups for support and occasional celebration.

EP.   I could swing with that. It would be a place for me to use my teaching and group skills while still holding a secular job!

A.   I would like to get you and a few other ex-pastors who live in this city together to talk about this. Each of you could convene a house church. In the meantime, you could meet together for additional training and mutual support. Your house groups could function under either ecumenical or denominational sponsorship.

EP.   Hey, I'd be a tentmaker minister, right?

A.   Right!

Between an advocate and a lay leader.

ADVOCATE: What about the church concerns you most?

LAY LEADER: Apathy. We just can't draw the crowds anymore. Recruiting people to work and teach is like pulling teeth. Our budget also reflects this apathy.

A.   Why is there apathy?

LL.   A variety of reasons, I suppose, but mostly a crisis of faith. People are less sure about what they believe and the church is less sure about what it should do. People either drop out or they stay but only go through the motions.

A.   Is there any way out?

LL.   If we could challenge people with something worthy of their best gifts and energies, they would respond. Routine bores them, and you can't motivate them with a "you ought to" tirade. If we could just hold up a vision and then free them to respond to the vision creatively.

A.   Sounds like you've thought seriously about this matter.

LL. You'd better believe it!

A.   Well, so have I, and I think that our times call for new and diverse forms of the church.

LL. How do you mean?

A.   No single task or vision can command the full attention of the church. There are myriad tasks. Our congregational patterns have emphasized uniformity — with everyone marching in lock step behind the pastor in a cause of his choosing. Today the church cannot afford to limit itself to one major concern; its mission style must be pluralistic. You lay leaders have a wealth of diverse concerns and gifts, and you should get in touch with them and organize around them. The problem of apathy would be whipped, for you would be acting upon the concern and gifts which are closer to you.

LL. That would take some doing!

A.   That is where the base church comes in. By establishing a variety of these small, base communities, you would provide both a setting for the discovery of gifts and a support cadre for their expression. The mood of our times calls for diverse, participatory styles.

LL. I see that, but what about those people who do not? I'm concerned for them, too. They are comfortable with their passive roles. They want to remain in their hiding places.

A.   They shouldn't be pushed. Traditional forms will have to be maintained, but you would be creating options for those who are hungry for new experiences.

LL. The house church sounds okay, but what do we do with our buildings? We have lots of money tied up in them.

A.   They can be used, although some remodeling may be necessary.

LL. We've got to stop the downward slide, all right, but we will need a lot of help. House churches are foreign to us, you know.

A. Yes, I know! But there are people who are eager to help.

Between an advocate and a dropout.

ADVOCATE: Tell me about your pilgrimage through the church.

DROPOUT: It's the typical story. I was raised in the church. I joined at age twelve, participated in youth activities, then went away to college and got away from the church. After my marriage and the arrival of our first child, I returned. The kids went to church school and we participated in men's and women's activities, plus other activities — for example, we belonged to the church bowling team. But then we moved, and we just didn't get active again. We visited some churches, but didn't find them warm. The kids are older now and they don't want to go anymore. Breaking into a sea of strangers isn't worth the effort.

A. Is that all?

DO. No. To be honest, I would have to say that God is not real to us. The words I learned in Sunday School — "faith," "salvation," "redemption" — they're foreign to my real world. Besides, the church seemed too busy with things other than my questions about faith and belief. Church became a bore.

A. If the church were really alive to your needs, what would it look like?

DO. In the first place, it should be small enough so that I couldn't get lost. I want people to know who I am, what I think, and how I feel. I would like to feel free enough to articulate my struggles and doubts without feeling stupid or getting put down. And I would like to know other people. I'd like to put my energy into helping people who hurt rather than working just to keep the ship called church afloat.

A. I believe this kind of church exists.

DO. Where?

A.   In a new, emerging form called "base church." Not many
      of these house churches exist, but people are showing
      interest.

DO. Do they shove their God down your throat?

A.   Generally not, but they do pray and worship. I think they
      will accept you where you are. You might rediscover some
      of the Sunday School words that bug you. They might take
      on real meaning for you in a loving community of faith.

DO. Okay, you tell me where one is. I'll give the church one
      more try.

A.   Come and see!

APPENDIX A

Instruction Sheet

Subgroup Analysis — Congregational Efficiency

This instrument will enable you to take a penetrating look at the subgroup structure of your congregation. It measures the efficiency of the congregation based upon the number and vitality of the subgroups in comparison with the communicant membership.

1. Identify on Form A and list by name all of the subgroups in your congregation. Include:

   Church School classes of *communicant* members
   Official Boards
   Committees and Task Forces
   Mission Groups, Social, Recreational Groups
   Prayer, Growth or Study Groups
   Circles
   Choir

   List any groups that have a life span of at least 3 meetings.

2. Record the number of meetings per month.

3. Record the average attendance.

4. Using Form B as a guide, record in each of the nine columns on Form A a number (from 0 to 10) which most closely reflects the group's effective life.

5. Add the horizontal columns and record the total in the right-hand column (maximum score = 90), then add the right-hand totals and record the grand total here _____. Also add the vertical columns and record them under "sub totals" for a profile picture of the functions.

6. Score the subgroup efficiency of your congregation as follows:

   Communicant membership of the congregation _____
   divided by 12 = _____
   times 90 = _____
   divided *into* the grand total of _____
   and multiplied by 100
   equals _____ % efficiency

FORM A

SUBGROUPS	Meetings Per Month	Average Attendance	FUNCTIONS									TOTAL
			Pray	Study	Worship	Tend	Disclose	Share	Explore	Strategize	Act	
SUB TOTALS												
GRAND TOTAL												

FORM B

SUBGROUP FUNCTIONS

SCALE — <u>1   2   3   4   5   6   7   8   9   10</u>
           Not Effective   Effective

KERYGMA

1. Pray — for each other, the church, and the world.
2. Study — the Biblical, historical, and theological tradition.
3. Worship — with focus upon the love, power, and grace of God.

KOINONIA

4. Tend — include, appreciate, listen to, and care for each other.
5. Disclose — personal feelings and thoughts, hopes and fears.
6. Share — material possessions (to some degree).

DIACONIA

7. Explore — issues and needs focused outside the group which might lead to corporate pronouncement or action.
8. Strategize — plan, practice, train, evaluate.
9. Act — doing work, tasks, ministry for the benefit of others beyond the group.

APPENDIX B

Shalom

A Personal Account of a House Church Experience

Charles M. Olsen

In the late afternoon each Sunday, our family room turned into a beehive of activity. All of the furniture was moved out, the carpet was vacuumed, and a table was constructed by placing a door on four one-gallon paint cans in the center of the floor. A tablecloth covered the door. Pillows were scattered around, candles were lighted, and fresh, homemade bread, and other simple, pot-luck foods were placed on the table. We were ready to host our "shalom" group — an experiment in house-church learning, fellowship, and worship. (Shalom means "peace," "health," "well-being.")

Within minutes, the room was full of people — five families in all, including fifteen children, all under age thirteen. Everyone sat on the floor. A guitar beckoned the group to share in a few gathering songs. Then during the singing of "Let us break bread together," people clustered around the table on their knees. As the fresh bread was broken and passed around, each person spoke a personal word.

"I'm thankful for my friend Greg," said Chuckie. "I pray that God's love will be known in and through us," said Bev. Bill shared a word about what caring people meant to him — especially the love of his wife, Bonnie. And so it went. A three-year-old broke bread with an adult. Brother shared with sister, friend with friend.

And who were these families? They were typical mobile families of Metropolitan Atlanta. One family had returned from Spain, another from Brazil. Home was Kansas, Kentucky, Alabama, Florida, New York, and Tennessee. Except for their immediate families, none had relatives living in Georgia. All had learned that when you move around, you have to make "family."

All of us were active participants in local congregations, but we wanted more than our parish programs offered. We were concerned about the way the church split us up. Children were placed in graded church-school classes. Women were recruited for "women's work." We wanted to participate in an intimate, caring "extended family" where we could gather with brother, sister, aunt, uncle, and cousin figures.

Our objective was to provide a context in which nurture, fellowship, and worship could take place. We felt that intergenerational and experience-based learning was a possibility which the church had not fully explored. My wife and I had participated in many small groups for couples, leaving the children with a babysitter. But children need to be in on some adult agendas, and adults desperately need to listen to and learn from children.

Worship in the traditional setting tends to be passive, whereas the shalom group provided an opportunity for shared prayers, praise, and reflections. Our behavior varied; sometimes it was unpredictable! The theme for each meeting was a single word — "friend," "love," "anger," "joy," "pain," "patience," "celebration." Everything — the bread-breaking, the selected scripture, the songs — touched on the theme. Around that word we shared, prayed, sang, danced, discussed, played, made things, and did role-playing.

A favorite activity was to engage reconstituted "families" in role-playing, with no two members of the same family in one group. Each person experienced relating to a new parent or child or sibling figure. Each learned by observing behavioral relationships with the new family.

One evening, for instance, a new family created a play around the theme "anger." The husband came home from work and dumped his load of woes upon the oldest child, who, in turn, "hung one on" the middle child, who then vented his feelings upon the youngest, a seven-year-old. The youngest child observed the "passing-it-on" phenomenon. Hands on hips, he complained, "But who do I have who is littler than me to get mad at?" Then he spied a toy dog (a planted prop) and he kicked it all the way across the room!

Shared prayers became an integral part of our life style. The little people could hardly sit still for a "pastoral" prayer or even sentence prayers. We found one-word or one-phrase "bombardment" type prayers to be the most effective — the little ones were not intimidated. Touching frequently accompanied the prayers, and often we prayed with our eyes open.

One evening we were struggling to find a way to express intercessory prayers which would evidence support and care for each person. We hit upon the "cradling" exercise, in which the subject is lifted to waist height by the whole group and rocked like a baby. During the cradling, we spoke personal words of appreciation, thanks, or encouragement — for example, "My prayer for you is —." The children insisted that the adults, too, be "rocked like a baby."

We grew so that physical closeness became a natural part of shalom. Holding hands, hugging, huddling, and cradling reinforced the expression of family.

After six months of meeting every Sunday, growing conflicts with local church activities brought a change in meeting patterns. Additionally, the adult agenda could not be dealt with in the family setting and in the ten to fifteen minutes that were available while the children were engaged in play outside the group. During the last three months of the experiment, the adults met together later on Sunday evenings two to three weeks per month, and with total families about once or twice a month. The adult shalom proved to be just as significant. Conducted in an unstructured way, it afforded growth via the path of openness, love, trust, and prayer. Fears, inadequacies, vocational decisions, search for meaning, and values were openly shared.

One evening, the conversation wandered from "A to Z" without really locking onto anything. Then, a participant who was at the door ready to leave, said, "By the way, what would you think of me if I no longer worked for the YMCA?" Needless to say, the meeting did not end there! Over a period of weeks, a supportive bond was formed around him while he was making a vocational decision.

Outside persons enriched the shalom gatherings. Mike, a black Presbyterian minister from Miami, shared openly the meaning of "blackness" and "whiteness" in our society. Brother Frank, from the Taizé Community in France, shared insights from his own experience of what it means to live in "community." When he affirmed that real community is "experienced in the context of resurrection faith," we paused to look back on our time together and to reflect on the ways in which our life together was lived in resurrection faith. We recalled experiences of open-ness, risk, and self-death in the group — of relationships of healing and restoring — of Christ being real through this body of his people!

When, finally, we evaluated our shalom experiment, we gleaned the following insights:

1. Intergenerational experiences have great value for the church; yet, our particular group had too many little people for it to function efficiently. We would have been strengthened by the presence of teens and older adults, including grandparent figures. The presence of college girls on occasion was beneficial.

2. Both the adult and intergenerational group experiences were valuable. A feasible pattern would have been for the adults to meet alone alternate weeks, including the children in between.

3. People can profit from highly participatory nurture and worship events.

4. The breaking of bread was the single most important event for the group, and especially for the children. The love feast, or agape meal, is a most appropriate setting for worship.

5. The "on the floor" informality fostered expression and participation in a way that "chairs in rows" could not have done. The setting has a vital bearing on goals, process, and achievement.

6. Extended families formed rapidly. The form provided an opportunity to get in quick, go in deep, and get out quick.

7. Terminating was a painful experience. Extended vacations,

a move by one of the families, and other emerging commitments signaled the end of the group as an ongoing weekly discipline. In terminating such a group, the grief process should be recognized and ways found to disband with thanks and celebration, rather than "winding down" and "petering out."

8. The church desperately needs to create and legitimate new and alternate forms of community, both within and outside the established congregation.

Our "shalom" will never end. It is a part of our family history and a clue to our future style.

Hey! Jesus and the twelve — and those first-century house-church Christians — were really onto something!

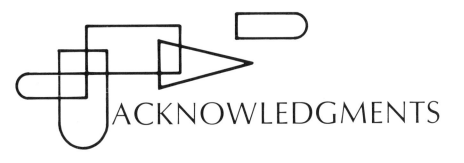

ACKNOWLEDGMENTS

Book Page

2   Selected material from personal correspondence. Reprinted by permission of The Institute of Church Renewal.

8,10,11   From *The Misunderstanding of the Church* by Emil Brunner. © 1952. Reprinted by permission of The Lutterworth Press.

9,22,23 24,26,27   From the *Today's English Version of the New Testament*. Copyright © American Bible Society 1966, 1971.

11,12   From *New Life in the Church* by Robert Raines. © 1961. Reprinted by permission of Harper and Row, Publishers.

12   From *Fire In Coventry* by Stephen Verney. © 1964. Reprinted by permission of Fleming H. Revell Company.

12,13   From *Rocking the Ark* by Grace Ann Goodman. © 1968, The Board of National Ministries. Reprinted by permission of the United Presbyterian Church in the U.S.A., Department of Mission Interpretation.

23   From *Alternative To Futility* by Elton Trueblood. © 1948. Reprinted by permission of Harper and Row, Publishers.

29,99, 130   From *Open House* by John Tanburn. Copyright © 1970. Reprinted by permission of The Falcon Press.